THE THEATRIC TOURIST

BY JAMES WINSTON

*A facsimile of the first and only edition of 1805
preceded by a facsimile of the original prospectus*

EDITED BY IAIN MACKINTOSH
WITH AN INTRODUCTION BY MARCUS RISDELL

THE SOCIETY FOR THEATRE RESEARCH
AND
THE BRITISH LIBRARY

2008

First published in 2008 by
The Society for Theatre Research
P.O. Box 53971
London SW15 6UL
www.str.org.uk

and

The British Library
96 Euston Road
London NW1 2DB
www.bl.uk

British Library Cataloguing in Publication Data
A CIP Record for this book is available from The British Library

ISBN 978 0 7123 5015 0 ✓

Designed by Bobby&Co, London
Printed and bound in England at the University Press, Cambridge

This facsimile is taken from pages selected from copies belonging to The British Library (78 l. 15), The Victoria
& Albert Museum Theatre Collections, Theat*research* – historic theatre consultants, and The Garrick Club.
Grateful thanks are given to the owners for giving their permission to reproduce the images. The cover design is
taken from the engraving of the *THEATRE, BIRMINGHAM* facing page 57 of *The Theatric Tourist*. The endpapers
are based on the original binding of the copy which was the property of James Winston and is now in the library
of The Garrick Club. The prospectus belongs to The British Library (937 g. 96). The portrait of James Winston is
an engraving by William Ridley, said to be 'from a fine miniature' by an unknown artist. It was published by
Vernor & Hood, Poultry, 31 August 1805, together with a biographical sketch, in *The Monthly Mirror* Volume XX.
It is reproduced by permission of the ArtArchive/Garrick Club.

The Society for Theatre Research was founded in 1948 by Ifan Kyrle Fletcher, Sybil Rosenfeld, Richard
Southern, George Speaight and others. It brings together those interested in the history and techniques of the
British theatre and encourages research into these subjects. Lectures are held in London and members receive
the Society's colour-illustrated journal, *Theatre Notebook*, and at least one book annually. In 2008 an international
conference 'The Georgian Playhouse and its Continental Counterparts 1750-1850' was held at the 1788 Georgian
Theatre Royal in Richmond, Yorkshire, as part of the celebrations of the 60th anniversary of the Society.
This volume marked the occasion.

Under the Patronage of Her Serene Highness

The Margravine of ANSPACH,

By whose Permission, an Engraving of her elegant Theatre, will be given as
a Frontispiece to the Publication.

———

PROSPECTUS

OF A WORK

(Never before presented to the Public,)

ENTITLED

THE THEATRIC TOURIST;

BEING A GENUINE COLLECTION OF CORRECT VIEWS,

WITH

BRIEF AND AUTHENTIC HISTORICAL ACCOUNTS

OF ALL THE

PRINCIPAL PROVINCIAL THEATRES

IN THE

UNITED KINGDOM.

———

BY A THEATRICAL AMATEUR.

Advertisement.

THIS Publication is introduced as a Candidate for Public Patronage under the following circumstances:

The Proprietor having for a series of Years, cultivated an early genius for the Pencil, amused himself in his Summer Excursions through the various Watering Places, Towns, &c. of the Kingdom, with making accurate Drawings of such Theatres as were ever rendered at all conspicuous by contributing to the rational gratification of a generous and discerning Public, and with collecting such established Facts concerning them, as were curious, useful and entertaining. As they were occasionally submitted to the inspection of his Friends, it was suggested that a Work of such a Nature, conducted on a liberal and extensive Scale would speedily form too valuable a Treasure to lie buried in the narrow precinct of a Portfolio, or a Drawing Book. It is to this flattering opinion that the THEATRIC TOURIST stands indebted for its promised existence; the Proprietor resolving to extend his labours and his influence to secure to his Production every possible success.

PROOFALS OF PUBLICATION.

PROPOSALS OF PUBLICATION.

THIS Work will be published monthly in not more than Thirty Numbers, at Three Shillings each, consisting of Three Views of principal Provincial Theatres, with at least Eight Pages of Letter-press, on fine paper, with a new type cast expressly for the purpose, containing an Historical Account of each View, collected from such Documents as leave no doubt of their authenticity and correctness; interspersed with occasional Anecdotes of the Managers of many of the Theatres, rendering it unexceptionably useful to Professors, and entertaining to the Curious.

The Plates to be nine inches and a half by six and three-quarters, *Engraved* and *Coloured* by the most eminent Artists.

Subscribers will be entitled every Sixth Number to an additional Plate, comprizing two or more Views of inferior Theatres.

A limited portion of Sets to be struck off, containing Proof Impressions of the Plates, with superior Embellishments, at Five Shillings per Number, on royal wove paper, hot-pressed.

The price to Non Subscribers will be advanced Sixpence each Number.

Subscribers to pay for one Number on entering their Names; and for the others on delivery, EXCEPT THE LAST.

In the last Number will be delivered a List of the Subscribers.

The accounts to be extended to those Theatres which from their confined situation cannot be subject to any sketch.

The First Number will be peremptorily ready for delivery on the 1st of MARCH 1804.

The Proprietor's more immediate aim being simply to cover his Expences, as may be gathered from the lowness of his Terms in the preceding Plan; and the encouragement he has already experienced, exceeding his most sanguine expectations, the Subscribers may rest assured that no considerations can induce him to publish the subsequent Numbers in a manner inferior to the first Specimen, either in paper, type, colouring or engraving. And it is with much satisfaction the Proprietor informs his Friends, Subscribers, and the Public, that the Plates are in such a state of present forwardness as to preclude the possibility of disappointment with regard to regularity of delivery.

Subscriptions will be received by C. Hughes, 5, Wigmore Street, Oxford Road; Vernon and Hood, Poultry; H. D. Symonds, Pater-noster Row; C. Chapple, 66, Pall Mall and 30 Southampton Row, Russel Square; by all the principal Booksellers in Town and Country, and by T. WOODFALL, Printer, No. 21, Villiers'-street, Strand, to whom all communications to the Editor (post-paid) are to be addressed.

The Proprietor of this Work has to thank his numerous Correspondents for many favours already received, which, with all future Communications will, in due time, be particularly acknowledged.

JAMES WINSTON & *THE THEATRIC TOURIST*

The Theatric Tourist of 1805 is doubly rare: not only have very few copies survived, but it is the only account of British theatre compiled by a man who was both actor and manager as well as author and artist. Until now, it has never been reprinted.

James Winston was born James Bown on 29th October 1773 in New Street, Covent Garden. His parents were Peter Bown, a hosier, and Elizabeth (née Winston), who had married on 12th January 1773. Whilst his mother died on 14th February 1789, his father did not pass away until 1823, somewhat contradicting the claim in *The Monthly Mirror* for August 1805 that he was orphaned as a child.

On 14th April 1795 his maternal grandfather died, leaving James Bown the sole heir of a substantial inheritance. In order to collect it he had to change his name to Winston by Royal Licence.

Presumably it was this inheritance which enabled Winston, using the assumed name James Neville, to become proprietor at the Richmond Theatre, Surrey in 1799. By now he had married the actress Frances Mary Villars, who appeared alongside him on the playbills. Winston explains in *The Theatric Tourist* [page 26] his purpose in taking on Richmond: 'to bring forward a set of actors, whose merits had been tried, and generally approved of, at the Private Theatre in *Tottenham-Court Road'*. Winston had been involved with that theatre between 1793 and 1796. Unfortunately he records that the season was full of 'losses and disappointments', this despite (or perhaps because of) his success with 'that *maker* of managers, PIZARRO, got up at great and unnecessary expense, (upwards of £200; uncommon for the country)'.

Following his ill fortune at Richmond, he and his wife appear on various bills in the provinces, their strolling taking them to Weymouth, Cheltenham, Margate and Plymouth. At the latter he became joint owner in 1803 and the following year he supervised its refitting. In *The Theatric Tourist* he recalls [page 69]: 'the whole of the interior... was rebuilt under the immediate and sole direction of, and from a drawing made by, Mr. WINSTON' before adding with some pride: 'as perfectly complete as any out of *London'*.

However his ambitions most certainly looked *towards* London. On 1st March 1802 he had written and appeared in a musical farce entitled *Perserverance; or, He Must Have Her* for an out of season benefit for the composer Walter Jones at the Haymarket Theatre. He himself played the five main characters.

It was at this point in his career that *The Theatric Tourist* was published, the first issue appearing on 1st March 1804. From an undated prospectus that has only recently come to light (illustrated opposite), we learn that he had 'for a series of years, cultivated an early genius for the Pencil, amused himself in his Summer Excursions through the various Watering Places, Towns, &c of the Kingdom, with making accurate Drawings of such Theatres as were rendered at all conspicuous by contributing to the rational gratification of a generous and discerning Public'. Not only do we find Winston establishing himself as the original artist for the plates, but we discover for the first time the full extent of his ambitions. He originally intended to publish 90 of these, with 'an additional Plate, comprising two or more Views of inferior Theatres' accompanying every sixth number. Indeed drawings, together with historical notes, anecdotes and accounts, can be found in numerous collections around the world for a total of nearly 300 theatres. Unfortunately by April 1805, when he was forced to close the subscription for financial reasons, only 24 had appeared in eight part works. In a notice 'To the Public' that accompanied the final issue, he announced that he had 'completed his collection of drawings' and offered them up for inspection by his subscribers at Wright & Co's Fashionable Repository. Also included was a title page so that they may at least 'bind up the numbers already published which form the first volume'. If there was an intention to recommence the subscription with further volumes at a later date, no more were forthcoming; furthermore no 'bound up' volume of the periodicals has yet come to light. A monograph containing the same 24 plates followed in Autumn the same year: extremely rare today, it is this 1805 volume of which this is a facsimile. An announcement appeared together with a biographical sketch and portrait of the author in *The Monthly Mirror* for August; the forthcoming volume was to include 'drawings of every public country theatre worthy of observation, which owe their correctness to the execution of this gentleman'. Furthermore it boasts that 'he [Winston] not only indulged a penchant for the drama, but the specimens he has given of the performance of his pencil, have proved

that his abilities at design are far from contemptible'. The literary style is idiosyncratic, a reflection not only of the diverse sources brought together by Winston the theatre antiquarian, but also a result of the florid style of his editor Edward J Longley. As a part-account of the Georgian playhouse in its golden age *The Theatric Tourist* is both invaluable and entertaining.

Winston then set aside *The Theatric Tourist* having just obtained a 1/8th interest in the Haymarket Theatre. Whilst he acted there throughout the 1805-1807 seasons, he rarely played the same part more than once and quickly took on a managerial role. Through his association with Robert William Elliston, first at the Surrey Theatre, then the Olympic, he became manager at Theatre Royal Drury Lane for the years 1819-1826. Now at the epicentre of London theatrical life, he was witness to all its goings-on, many of which he recorded in his diary (selections of which were published by the Society for Theatre Research in 1974). In fact his knowledge of all things dramatic was called upon by the *Select Committee on Dramatic Literature* to which he was called to testify in June 1832. When asked by its chair Edward Bulwer-Lytton 'what do you think is meant by the regular drama?' he concluded that if a theatre is allowed to 'play everything, everything is the regular drama'. However, when pressed with the question 'is horsemanship the regular drama, or lions?' he responded 'No, I should consider not; not lions, certainly'. A lion, tiger and four zebras had recently been presented at Astley's Amphitheatre.

In the months running up to his testifying to the Select Committee he had been a driving force behind the founding of the Garrick Club. Together with Samuel Arnold of the Lyceum Theatre and the playwright architect Samuel Beazley, joined by the old war hero Sir Andrew Barnard and the wealthy railway speculator Francis Mills, he has to be considered as one of the Club's founders since these five constituted the founding committee that met in Theatre Royal Drury Lane on 17th August 1831. Prior to the completion of its first Club House, all meetings took place at Winston's home at 3 Charles Street, Covent Garden and he was greatly influential in shaping its agenda and constitution. He would serve as the Club's first Secretary and Librarian until his death in 1843; his legacy is still felt there today.

MARCUS RISDELL

Librarian
The Garrick Club
May 2008

THE THEATRIC TOURIST;

BEING A GENUINE COLLECTION OF CORRECT VIEWS,

WITH

BRIEF AND AUTHENTIC HISTORICAL ACCOUNTS

OF ALL THE

PRINCIPAL PROVINCIAL THEATRES

IN THE

UNITED KINGDOM.

REPLETE WITH USEFUL AND NECESSARY INFORMATION TO THEATRICAL PROFESSORS, WHEREBY THEY MAY
LEARN HOW TO CHUSE AND REGULATE THEIR COUNTRY ENGAGEMENTS; AND WITH
NUMEROUS ANECDOTES TO AMUSE THE READER.

By A THEATRIC AMATEUR.

LONDON:

Printed by T. Woodfall, No. 21, Villiers-Street, Strand.

AND SOLD BY H. D. SYMONDS, PATERNOSTER-ROW; VERNOR and HOOD, POULTRY; LINDSELL, WIGMORE-STREET,
OXFORD-ROAD; E. KERBY, STAFFORD-STREET, BOND-STREET; SYLVESTER, STRAND;
C. CHAPPLE, NO. 66 PALL-MALL, AND NO. 30, SOUTHAMPTON-ROW,
RUSSELL-SQUARE; AND BY ALL THE PRINCIPAL
BOOKSELLERS IN TOWN AND COUNTRY.

1805.

BATH.

London, Published 1 March 1804 by T. Woodfall Villiers S¹ Strand.

THEATRE-ROYAL, BATH.

I<small>T</small> appears to be not only consistent with the nature of our design, but a compliment unquestionably due, to commence our researches with the history of that theatre, which boasts the most distinguished rank in public estimation, and we trust that no one will deem it an invidious distinction, that, next to *London*, *Bath* should be thought the favorite of the muses; particularly, as we presume not to *adjudge* the histrionic crown, but simply to *acknowledge* it, where shining the well earned meed of popular decision. No theatre has shone so conspicuously as a nursery for *London*, as this of *Bath*. The circumstance of its having brought so nearly to perfection a S<small>IDDONS</small>, E<small>DWIN</small>, H<small>ENDERSON</small>, and K<small>ING</small>, will always command respectful mention, while a genuine taste for dramatic excellence continues to exist. Indeed, in one respect, it were " a consummation devoutly to be wished," that *Bath* should dictate to the proud city of the Empire, nay, to the Christian world, its own tenaciousness of the character of those to whom it affords its patronage; for here an additional zest is spread among an audience, from a general presumption, that the personifier of virtue feels its genuine dictates, and that the mimic villain is the domestic husband and the respected man: at any rate, the *grossly profligate* is sure to be discountenanced.

D<small>RAMATIC</small> representations in this city are of early origin, though we are unable to trace any thing like an *established theatre*, further than the reign of C<small>HARLES</small> the Second; nor, indeed, uninterruptedly so long. About the close of the seventeenth century, the Earl of R<small>OCHESTER</small> happening to visit *Bath*, convinced the citizens of the improbability of the tale of B<small>LADUD</small> and his swine, (as discoverers of the salubrious property of its waters), and induced them to remove a memorandum of the circumstance, that was publicly exhibited. Some years after, Mr. P<small>OWELL</small> gave a mortal wound to the inconsistent legend, by associating B<small>LADUD</small> and his pigs with Punch and his merry

family

family on the stage. A play-house appears to have occupied the scite of the present General Hospital, and was in 1705 erected by the subscription of persons of the highest rank, who suffered their arms to be engraved upon the building, as a public testimony of their liberality towards it. In 1720, and for some years afterwards, WATKINS headed a travelling company in turn with others. About 1746, an itinerant troop, commanded by Mr. LINNETT, performed in a newly erected theatre in *Kingsmead Street*.

HITHERTO theatricals seem to have been entirely dependent on casualty, but in 1747, the comedian HIPPISLEY laid the foundation of a regular series, by making proposals for the construction of a commodious theatre, on account of the insufficiency of the play-room then in use. A building was accordingly begun, and actually carried on to a considerable degree of forwardness, when a check was suddenly put to the proceedings, by the death of their projector in the summer of the following year, while resident at *Bristol*. The stage, however, which in no age since ESCHYLUS and SOPHOCLES, has been without its partizans, found an effectual patron in the liberal and enterprizing spirit of JOHN PALMER, Esq. citizen and brewer, who, in 1750, assisted by the subscriptions of nine others, completed the theatre in *Orchard Street*, adjoining the parades. The principal part of these subscribers, soon after, disposed of their interest in the property to Mr. PALMER, in consequence of the proprietor of the old play-room having, in violation of agreement, opened in opposition; not caring to brave the issue of a contest, which Mr. PALMER ended. In 1753 or 4, Mr. SIMPSON conducted a sharing company in a theatre, the lower part of which was precisely the model of *Drury Lane*, with a stage much larger than that in *Orchard Street*. The two houses were once compelled to close for about three weeks, in consequence of an information lain against them, which proceeded to a process; but at length was over-ruled by the powerful support of the nobility and gentry, who were *hurt* at the restriction of their favourite amusement. Mrs. CHARKE, the unhappy daughter of COLLEY CIBBER, who as frequently appeared in man's as in her own attire, was SIMPSON's prompter: her picture of the company does not exhibit the most favorable idea of their merits; great altercations for preference of parts, and distinctions in the bills, owing to the weak good nature of the manager, who from unwillingness to give offence, even to the most insignificant performer, frequently resigned his right of authority, when under the greatest need of its exertion. Mrs. CHARKE declares, that when she has written for the printer the word *performed*, it would have been no error to have changed

it

it to *deformed.* This competition of the two theatres, was, after some time, finally adjusted, by the grant of an annual consideration to Mr. SIMPSON, who resigned in favor of his rival. Mr. KING, at this time, enjoyed the supremacy of the stage department. The theatre has since been enlarged and improved by the son of the original patentee, late comptroller of the post-office, and at present a representative in parliament for this his native city, under the direction and joint management of Mr. DIMOND. Previous to 1756, Mr. GENTLEMAN, and Copper Captain BROWN, successively presided at the helm of theatrical affairs, which in 1757 devolved to Mr. LEE, whose daughter wrote the celebrated Chapter of Accidents, to extricate him from some temporary embarrassments. Mr. LEE's superior eminence as a performer must remain on record, while the " Life of GARRICK" assigns him a salary of ten pounds per week, for the trouble of *receiving it;* though Mr. GARRICK was undoubtedly a man of *singular modesty,* never thinking his reputation completely safe, when contrasted with other than a PACKER or a BRANSBY. Mr. LEE having a difference with the proprietor, quitted his appointment; and in the summer of 1761 opened the *Winchester* Theatre, attracted by the prospect which a large camp afforded him. In 1758, the *Bath* comedians performed at *Newport,* in the *Isle of Wight,* from a similar inducement; but the waggon that conveyed the *properties,* was ignited on *Salisbury Plain,* and the private wardrobe of individuals, together with the public stock of bowls, daggers, skulls, bones, thunder, lightning, and a heavy fall of rain, were instantly consumed to ashes. To add to the misfortune, sudden orders breaking up the camp, the town was unable longer to support them; they, therefore, prudently retreated; but halting at *Reading,* remained till the *Bath* season summoned the wanderers home. Mr. HULL, had, at this time a share in the concern. In 1760, Mr. KEASBERRY, and Mr. GRIFFITH of the *Norwich* Theatre, succeeded. In 1761, Mr. ARTHUR, a great comic actor, and the best English clown, managed under Mr. PALMER, who had, by that time, become the sole proprietor. Mr. ARTHUR had built a theatre at *Portsmouth,* whither he took the company that and the following summer, as KEASBERRY and GRIFFITH had done the year before, to *Winchester.* He died in 1772. In 1766, the celebrated QUIN exchanged time for eternity, and was buried in the Abbey, on the 24th of June, aged 73. On the 26th of November, 1767, a bill was brought before the parliament, on petition of Mr. PALMER, the mayor, aldermen, and common council, (being the first of the kind in England), and after encountering many difficulties, at length happily passed through both houses, for the security of theatrical property. A patent was accordingly made out for twenty-one years, from the

25th

25th of March, 1768; at which time, Mr. LEE again was manager, retaining the situation till his death. Mr. HENDERSON appeared at *Bath*, in the character of Hamlet, on the 16th of October, 1772, during the management of Mr. PALMER, under the name of COURTNEY: he was a man of clumsy figure, but excellent understanding, though a great imitator of GARRICK. With all his disadvantages, he read and played the character better than any at present on the stage: he was engaged at a guinea per week, a dog's-day benefit, and the advantage of KEASBERRY to *teach him how to act*; however, experience and his own good sense, made him at last, from a servile mimic, a no less decided original. In 1787, the direction rested with Mr. KEASBERRY, who had become a patentee, and retained the management till his decease, assisted by Mr. DIMOND, who then reigned solely. Mr. DIMOND was bred to the business of a chaser: he made his *debut*, about nine and twenty years ago, at *Drury Lane*, in the character of Romeo, under the tuition of Mr. GARRICK; he shortly afterwards appeared at *Bath*, where his sobriety and mild demeanor procured him many friends, and he became as great a favorite as ELLISTON is at present. Having the good fortune to marry a woman of property, he purchased a share of the theatre; and there is not an actor in it that sits uneasy under his auspicious government. BLISSET, sometimes reminding him of former days, when they were unable to muster half-a-crown between them, asks him if he retains the shoes in which he entered *Bath*: they were fellow pedestrians, and BLISSETT feels a pride in keeping *his*. He is a singular character; but, understanding that his life is shortly to be published, we forbear to anticipate the items. We doubt not but that the work will amply repay the reader; for no man has seen more of theatrical hardships, particularly in *Ireland*, where, *Dublin* excepted, players are held in indifferent estimation. We are authorized, however, to state that he was born at *Reading*, in *Berkshire*, and was sent to seek his fortune at the tender age of thirteen, when, after trying various professions, he fixed on that of actor. He came out under the management of Mr. otherwise known by the name of BOBBY BATES, at *Shepton Mallet*, and was soon afterwards transferred to *Smock Alley*, *Dublin*. After following a variety of fortunes, he has at last retired on an independence of about two hundred pounds per annum. A few years ago, he intimated to Mr. DIMOND his intention of withdrawing from the company, unless an increase of salary was granted him. Mr. DIMOND reminded him, that he was in possession of the highest salary the theatre allowed, (three pounds a week), and he was confident the rule could not be broken; and moreover hinted that he was not in need of increase. " That may be,"

said

said BLISSETT, " but I must have it, or quit the theatre." The demand being
required, he stated *three shillings* weekly ; which, Mr. DIMOND declared, he
must pay out of his own pocket. This may suffice to prove the whim of his
character. An engagement was once settled for him at *Covent Garden*, at five
pounds a week, by the late Mr. WOODFALL; but he declined fulfilling it,
from an absolute fear of appearing in the capital ; and it was not without reluctance that he consented to perform last summer, at the *Hay-Market;* for
which he received a compensation of two hundred pounds.

THE year 1801 is memorable for the establishment of a theatrical fund, for the
relief of decayed actors ; being the only institution of the kind, *Norwich* excepted, out of *London*. A night is granted by the liberality of the manager,
towards the increase of it, at the latter end of each season ; though, in order
to ensure a capital commensurate to every probable claim, it is designed to
remain untouched till the expiration of seven years, from the time of its
establishment : to the credit of Mr. J. EDWIN, his name appears as the pro-
moter of so laudable a scheme. The season continues from the middle of
September to the latter end of July : for the first fortnight or three weeks,
they perform three nights at *Bristol*, (Monday, Wednesday, and Friday), and
one at *Bath* (on Saturday) ; afterwards, three nights at *Bath*, (Tuesday,
Thursday, and Saturday), and one at *Bristol* (Monday) : four nights, *occasionally*, in the Christmas week, and four at Easter. The box price, under the
management of Mr. PALMER, was 5s. being the highest terms for a constancy,
ever submitted to out of the metropolis. The admissions are at present,
boxes 4s. pit 2s. 6d. first gallery 1s. 6d. upper gallery 1s. The house will
hold from 140 to 145 pounds ; 160 with the pit laid into the boxes : expences,
at present thirty-five. The average receipts in full season, are from
eighty to ninety pounds ; more than £.3,000 are said to have been cleared
in the last year. Independently of the advantage of so long a season, the
performers are entitled to spring and winter benefits ; the first at *Bristol*, and
the last at *Bath*, which is the better by fifty or sixty pounds, and free con-
veyance for themselves and luggage, from theatre to theatre. Indeed, the
long coaches, or caterpillars, as they have been not unappropriately called, are said
to have been invented expressly for the purpose, though *Plymouth* contests
the claim, and challenges the credit of them for the use of the jolly tars.
Mr. WROUGHTON, Mrs. CRAWFORD, and Mr. HOARE, (the dramatic writer),
were born in this city.

c   MR.

Mr. Palmer united the interests of *Bath* and *Bristol*; the latter of which he now holds in conjunction with Mr. Dimond, by virtue of a lease which expires with the patent. A Mr. Charlton has been for several seasons appointed to the management, in relief of Mr. Dimond, a gentleman well calculated to render the situation of the performers every way agreeable. The present company, in point of merit, is far inferior to what has been repeatedly witnessed. There is no performer of any particular eminence, excepting Mr. Elliston, whose abilities have now been fairly tried and approved; but, as is too frequently the case when actors become established, he sometimes presumes on the favor of his audience by attempting characters, which he is by no means calculated to support : the range of the drama has been successfully compassed by Garrick only; and it is our wish to speak with due humility, while we declare our opinion, that, however such practices may exhibit a versatility of genius, it can only by reflecting persons be considered as a prostitution of their talents, for men to personify characters replete with every manly virtue and every moral sentiment, and immediately buffoon and contradict the very essence and spirit of their performance. The only thing that can be said in mitigation of this practice in country theatres, is, the necessity they are in some sort under to provide, what is technically termed, *useful hands.* Mr. Elliston made a trial at this theatre about twelve years ago, in the character of Tressel, in King Richard the Third ; but not procuring an engagement, he attempted *York,* from whence he shortly afterwards returned to *Bath.* He received the rudiments of a classical education in the grammar school in *St. Paul's Church-Yard;* and is certainly equal, if not superior, to the mass of modern actors.

The theatre is commodious and elegant; but we think the custom of using the lobby for a box-office, would be more " honored in the breach than the observance," for, notwithstanding the doors of the boxes are secured, it certainly hazards a disturbance of rehearsal. This department is under the able regulation of the father of Mr. Bartley, of *Drury Lane.* The great space allowed for the stage doors gives the frontispiece a heavy appearance, being more than double the customary dimensions. The auditory is semicircular : the whole designed and executed by Mr. Palmer, architect; and it reflects on his professional abilities, take it for all in all, considerable credit.

Benefits

BENEFITS on sharing plans are utterly excluded. The *Bath* performers receive no previous notice of dismissal, but are retained or discharged, according as they are found more or less useful, at the close of the season.

WE cannot close this account better, than by presenting to our readers the following lines, from under the bust of Mr. QUIN, (which bust is called a likeness of him in his latter days), being the happy effusion of our English ROSCIUS; and which are introduced as a Trio, by Mr. DIGNUM, among his " *Melodies*," which are honored with a longer list of subscribers, than almost any work extant.

" That tongue which set the table in a roar,
" And charm'd the public ear, is heard no more ;
" Clos'd are those eyes, the harbingers of wit,
" Which spake before the tongue what SHAKSPEARE writ:
" Cold is that hand, which living was stretch'd forth
" At friendship's call, to succour modest worth.
" Here lies JAMES QUIN ; deign reader to be taught,
" Whate'er thy strength of body, force of thought,
" In nature's happiest mould however cast,
" To this complection thou must come at last.

DESCRIPTION OF THE PLATE.

The first door is the avenue leading to the stage; the second to the galleries; and, the third the pit. The fourth was made about two or three years back, for the convenience of entering the boxes, it being found that two chairs were sufficient to block up the regular entrance, which is pointed out by the wide adjoining door. The sixth entrance is a private door appointed for chairs only, close to which, on the other side of the projection, may be seen the upper part of a passage to the boxes, intended for the convenience of carriages, coming by the way of St. James's Street : from the paved court you descend a few steps into another court, in which this door is situated.

THEATRE,

THEATRE, ANDOVER.

AS a foil to the Theatre of *Bath*, we proceed to give that of *Andover;* for, as *Bath* enjoys perhaps the most considerable share of public estimation, so *Andover* challenges the most deficient, in the leading points that usually obtain it. The name of the manager, (THORNTON; or, more properly, FORD), unhappily suffices to confirm the assertion. We have but little to observe respecting it, and think the less the better; for one of the offices of candour is to be silent, where it cannot commend; but, considering the nature of our engagement to the public, it becomes a part of duty to unfold the practices by which their liberality is frequently abused, as much as to display the excellencies which deserve their patronage. As Mr. THORNTON maintains so many theatres; or, rather as so many theatres contribute to the maintenance of Mr. THORNTON, we shall have frequent occasion to note his eccentricities, which are almost as many and as ludicrous as the celebrated WHITLEY's. This town, like most others of our manager's resort, has been adopted by him, when deserted by all other theatrical campaigners. SHATFORD of *Salisbury*, and COLLINS of *Winchester;* the former eighteen, and latter but sixteen miles from *Andover*, were afraid to venture a concern there; and had not the enterprizing THORNTON taken pity on the townsmen, they had probably had but transient glimpses of the sock and buskin. Mr. THORNTON is, however, particularly careful never to lose by any of his adventures, as his schemes are conducted on so confined a principle, that a nightly average of a few pounds will amply repay him; and but for his constant rage for building, must have long since realized a handsome independence. Upwards of thirty years ago, a Mr. BOWLES frequented *Andover*, but never exceeded once in two or three years, since which a Mr. HOUNSLOW *once* exhibited. These representations were generally carried on in a large malt-house, barn, or some such scene of action, till about eighteen years ago, the present manager ventured to rent a large thatched barn, on lease for ten years, at ten pounds per year, situate in the yard of the Angel Inn, after agreeing with the proprietor, (a carpenter by trade), to enlarge and make it fit, at a considerable expence: the

decorations

ANDOVER.

Publish'd 1 March, 1804, by T. Woodfall

decorations were better than could have been reasonably expected, and seemed tolerably well to answer; but, about the time the lease expired, sad to relate! the theatrical barn was sold, and falling into the hands of one of the people denominated quakers, who wanted it for other purposes, our Thespian General was so completely routed, as to be unable to rally till about Christmas, 1802; when, after meeting many disappointments, he happily succeeded, agreeing with Mr. RAWLINS, a printer, (who procured him permission to perform), to bestow an adequate rent for a long lease, on condition of Mr. RAWLINS's erecting the shell of a theatre at his own expence, which was begun soon after the 1st of January, 1803, and performed in the following Easter Monday. The interior was neatly fitted up by Mr. THORNTON, and holds from thirty to forty pounds. Boxes 3s. Upper Boxes 2s. 6d. Pit 2s. Gallery 1s. There is no regular season, the visitation depending on the will of the manager; whose intention, we understand, is to perform in it once in two years, at least. It stands in a dirty lane, leading from the upper end of *Andover* to *Newbury;* is on a small scale, but being new, has a clean appearance. Mr. RAWLINS having, it is said, improved this lane, it is now called *Rawlins's Place.* When we inspected the theatre, we might safely have exclaimed, " What a sweet place is this!" for Mr. RAWLINS, who is a general chapman, and who has a communication from his dwelling with the play-house, had completely filled a part of it with pots of *honey.* We shall find the idea further justified by a reference to the bottom of the bills, where we learn that places for the boxes are to be had at Mr. TREAKELL's. The company possess the happy art of producing more novelty than persons in general are aware of, for the spectators may constantly enjoy on the repetition of the same play, as *announced* in the public bills, a totally different performance. Sometime since, a new comedy being given out for an early representation, the performers had no time to perfect themselves in their respective characters: in short, they knew scarcely a syllable as printed; however, the night came; the last bell rung; the call-boy summoned the actors in the green-room:—hold, we forgot, call-boy and green-room are dramatic requisites, which our manager has hitherto thought too trifling to adopt. Mr. THORNTON examining the audience through the usual fissure in the curtain, observed a book in the hand of a gentleman in the boxes, which he could not but conjecture to be a *copy* of the *play.* What was to be done? A council of war was called upon the stage; one of the party not yet dressed, was dispatched into the box, and, on his return, confirmed the dread suspicion. With such a potent evidence of their incorrectness, it was impossible to proceed; time elapsed; the audience were clamorous; the

D   fiddles

fiddles weary: it was highly necessary that something should be immediately put in practice, and the following was adopted. The spectators, (the few who had assembled), were informed, with all the solemnity of deep concern, that the *prompt-book* having been unfortunately mislaid, was the sole occasion of this unusual procrastination. The gentleman alluded to, politely offered to accommodate them with the loan of his, hoping it would prove a tolerable succedaneum. This was the very thing they were in quest of :—the evidence dismissed, the performance was carried on with the utmost vivacity. It is somewhat singular that Mr. HATTON, whose abilities are certainly beyond mediocrity, should have remained so long in such a company. We do not speak from what we saw him in, last season, at the *Hay-Market;* for, there, he was more frequently out of his line, than otherwise. The circumstance of his being related to the manager, is probably the inducement.

DESCRIPTION OF THE PLATE.

The only entrance to the front of the theatre, is through the folding doors in the centre of the building. The arms over the semicircular blind window are neatly executed; but exhibit immediately beneath them a singular deception. To induce a belief of its being a patent theatre, the words " From the" are written so faintly, as to be scarcely legible, while " Theatre-Royal" appears in striking characters, followed by an almost invisible " Windsor."

THEATRE-

MARGATE.

London. Publish'd 1 March 1804, by T. Woodfall Villiers S.t Strand.

THEATRE-ROYAL, MARGATE.

IN 1762, one WILLIAM SMITH, a wool-comber of *Essex*, conducted the *Margate*, *Canterbury*, *Dover*, *Deal*, *Maidstone*, *Feversham*, and *Rochester* Theatres. The *first*, (under present consideration), was a barn, situated in a place known by the appellation of the *Dean*. This circuit he continued till the year 1768, when, for particular reasons, though much respected and encouraged, was forced to relinquish the East part of *Kent*, exhibiting only in the West. Availing himself of this necessity, THOMAS BURTON, ostler at the Ship, at *Feversham*, who used to snuff SMITH's candles, when his company performed there, assumed the reins of the theatrical government that his predecessor abdicated. This man had a daughter, who was deemed in these parts a star of considerable magnitude ; but, be it as it may, she contrived to procure an engagement at *Drury Lane*, and, after playing there two seasons, died at *Poole*, in *Dorsetshire*. The father also died in the year 1771, at the Hole in the Wall, at *Margate*. About this time WILLIAM BROWN, a currier, and JOHN RICHARDSON, a taylor, both of *Canterbury*, opened the theatre, which they had removed to a stable at the back of the Fountain Inn. BROWN retained the circuit till 1778, but RICHARDSON resigned, as will be fully stated in the *Canterbury* section. In 1779, CHARLES MATE assumed the managerial sceptre, of whom a number of whimsical stories are related. Having passed the early part of his life at sea, though possessed of a good understanding, he still retained the roughness of the element to which he had been bred. Nature had endued him with respectable talents as a *comic actor;* but, he was sadly deficient in the qualifications requisite for successful *management*, as will appear by the following well authenticated anecdote, which we insert, merely to give an idea of the man. While his company exhibited at *Sandwich*, a vain young fellow of the town, applied for permission to play the character of Hamlet. MATE, who knew about as much of tragedy as RICH, late patentee of *Covent Garden*, undertook to *instruct* him in this arduous part. The *Tyro* simply asked him, how he should *look* on the appearance of the Ghost ?—
" Look ?"

" Look ?" said the tutor, with more bluntness than misconception, " look !
why, you must *look*—as much as to say, D—n my eyes, here's a rig !" He
rented of Mr. Cobb, then banker and magistrate, at *Margate*, upon lease, at twenty pounds per season, (expending about £.200 in the fitting up) a large stable
behind the Fountain Inn.   The building was sixty-five feet in length,
twenty-five of which he converted into a raised stage, and the remainder
into box, pit, and gallery.   What was very singular, the pit of other theatres
was the boxes of that, and *vice versa*.   Notwithstanding the neighing of
horses, and yelping of dogs in the stable, over which the stage was built,
the place occasionally overflowed with the best company ; but, the most
absurd and remarkable part of the business was, the performers coming
to the front of the house in the public street, in their tragic and comic robes,
with powdered heads and painted faces, till they had a sufficient number of au-
ditors to pay their night's expences, when ALEXANDER and his lovely STATIRA,
with all their train of attendants, would retire in good order, to display their
several talents to the best of their abilities.   Boxes 3s. pit 2s. and gallery 1s.
held three and thirty pounds, and was conducted on a sharing scheme. He
kept the circuit uninterruptedly till 1784, when Mrs. BAKER, whom we shall
frequently have occasion to introduce to public notice, commenced an opposition.   She applied to Mr. COBB for permission to erect a theatre on a superior
plan ; but COBB, as proprietor of the old concern, naturally gave a decided ne-
gative ; whereupon the *gentle fair one* entered a remonstrance, and declared
her right to murder SHAKSPEARE equally with MATE ; and told him, for all he
was a Justice, she would build in spite of him.   Accordingly, the following
year produced a *Baker's company*, who exercised their calling near the church,
and instituted a theatrical warfare.   This must have proved an annihilating
system to one of the belligerent powers, but for the interference of the magistrate, the mandates of whom had been so lightly regarded ; nevertheless, MATE,
for the present, experienced an overthrow, and had nearly left the field to the
victorious *Thalestris ;* when, on the 6th of August, a convention of the parish-
ioners was called by Mr. COBB, who entreated them to sign a petition that
MATE had prepared, to send to parliament, for the procuration of a patent.
The success of the appeal was such, that by the close of evening, the signatures
of no less than 907 persons appeared in support of the proceeding.   Mr.
ROBSON, who was at that time an inhabitant of *Margate*, came forward to
assist MATE in the prosecution of his project.   Mr. ROBSON having been about
thirty years ago, a singer of some eminence at *Covent Garden*, afterwards at

Norwich,

Norwich, York, and other provincial theatres) and MATE finding the expence, trouble, &c. too much for an individual like him, proposed to Mr. ROBSON a joint interest in the scheme, which with reluctance he at length acceded to. Thus strengthened, he applied to Sir JAMES LUTTERELL, one of the representatives of *Dover*, who so far espoused his cause, as to solicit the Prince of WALES and the Metropolitan of CANTERBURY to forward the petition, which passed both Houses with much trouble, and an expence of £.550, in the face of a counter-petition, that being unsupported, died naturally away. By virtue of the patent (which limits the performance from the 1st of May to the 31st of October), they re-opened, and saw an order issued from the Chamberlain's office for the suspension of Mrs. BAKER's opposition. In consequence, she struck her theatre, which was a temporary wooden structure, and transported it to *Feversham*. Thus rid of their opponent, they purchased a piece of ground for £.80, in order to erect a more respectable edifice. The foundation stone, bearing the following inscription, was laid on the 19th of September, 1786, in the presence of near five thousand persons.

" This first stone for a Theatre-Royal, was laid in due form, attended by the brethren of the *Thanet* Lodge, by the proprietors, THOMAS ROBSON and CHARLES MATE, the 21st of September, A. D. 1786—A. L. 5786, in the reign of King GEORGE the Third.—Duke of CUMBERLAND, Grand-Master."

The ceremony was attended by the free-masons of *Margate*, &c. in honour of ROBSON, Master of the Lodge, who sung several masonic songs, accompanied by a band of music ; and who addressed the populace in a nervous and appropriate speech, amidst their general acclamations.

This Theatre, which cost about £.3000, was opened the 27th of June, 1787, with She Stoops to Conquer, and, All the World's a Stage. An occasional prologue from the pen of M. P. ANDREWS, Esq. was delivered by the late Mr. BOOTH, to whom Mr. ROBSON disposed of half his moiety for £.1000.

The natural easiness of Mr. MATE's disposition, rendered it necessary that Mr. ROBSON should be invested with the management; and, the better, to ensure his forbearance, bound himself in a penalty of £.500. In 1790, ROBSON, without the privity of his colleague, sold his remaining share to Mr. KING, of *King-Street, Covent-Garden*, for £.900, on which, poor MATE was inconsolable ; his words are, " I lost my right hand, for I here declare,

D

declare, no man was ever better calculated for a scheme of this nature, for he was endued with *honour, truth,* and *justice.*" Mr. GRUBB, one of the proprietors of *Drury-Lane,* who was play mad, sent to MATE, at this juncture playing in BERNARD's company at *Guernsey,* to treat for his portion of the *Margate* Theatre. Agreeing to the proposals, he relinquished his title, on receiving a consideration of £.2,200, and now exercises his professional talents in the *Dover* company. The Fort Major of *Sheerness* bespoke the play of Cato, CHARLES MATE was the Sempronius—who procured of the Major seven super-numeraries, to have the play done in style, as he called it. Six were very tractable, but the seventh, a drummer, dressed in a soldier's old coat, with a large buff belt buckled round his waist, notwithstanding MATE's instructions, that at the words, " See the unhappy men, they weep !" they were to appear to do so, kept nodding to his old friends in the gallery, and grinning through-out the scene. RICHARDSON, who played Cato, vexed at his conduct, in addition to " Sempronius, see they suffer death !" said, " but for that fellow in the buff belt, let him have all the torments can be felt." The Fort Major on his return examined the play, and not finding the last couplet, banished the company from *Sheerness,* and they remained out of bread for three weeks.

Mr. GRUBB has frequently performed for public charities. Mr. WILMOT WELLS was appointed manager by the new proprietors; and, Mr. HULL, in 1792, conducted the stage department. Mr. KING lived to enjoy his purchase but little better than a year; when an eighth was disposed of to Mr. SHAW of *Covent-Garden,* to superintend the orchestra; but, shortly after dying, his brother of *Drury-Lane* succeeded to the share.

Mrs. BOOTH, relict of the joint proprietor, who died in 1788, having ad-ministered to her husband's will, became, of course, responsible for all his debts, which she contrived to liquidate within £.100. To provide for this deficiency, she made over to Mr. WELLS her interest in the share, till her son should become of age, and capable of claiming his father's legacy, for the advance of the required means : Mrs. BOOTH was a performer in the company, but at this period dismissed. Mr. RUSSELL had the management in the summer of 1798. The Theatre generally opens about the second Monday in July, and closes in October. The wardrobe is barely passable, and the dressing rooms so distant from the stage, as to occasion much delay between the acts and pieces, especially when change of dress is requisite. When the House was built, a green room was totally forgotten—there is now an attempt to rectify the error, in a corner of the stage, about six or eight feet square, but being

being a thoroughfare for players, scene-shifters, &c. its utility is rendered almost ineffectual. The scenery is excellent. Admission prices are, Boxes 4s. Pit 2s. 6d. and Gallery 1s. but when performers of eminence appear for a few nights only, they are advanced to 5s. 3s. and 1s. 6d. Half price, so utterly destructive to the business of a theatre, is here with great propriety rejected. The House will hold about £.80, at the accustomed terms, *two* seats having been added to the pit, (the price of which before was 2s.), and *one* to the boxes, by taking in a part of the side lobbies, both above and below. Benefit charges twenty guineas. Two or three masquerades have been introduced within these few years, in the course of every season; for which purpose, a temporary flooring has been constructed for the pit. The wings being removed, a range of columns representing Sienna marble, terminates semicircularly, and with the assistance of some scenery, chandeliers, &c. composes a picturesque saloon. The only entrance is through the center box, the front of which is taken down on the occasion. To the number of near four hundred, the company are indiscriminately admitted, whether masked or not. The woeful inconvenience of dividing the property of a theatre into many shares, has been severely felt at *Margate*; at one time no less than *sixteen ladies* having been quartered on the groaning treasury. We understand some trifling alterations have lately occurred in the disposition of the shares, and others are speedily expected. A Mrs. HENRY, and Mr. RUSSELL, mentioned in the preceding page, appear as partners in the firm. A project is in contemplation for uniting the theatre of *Margate* with that of *Dover*, and others in the neighbourhood.

DESCRIPTION OF THE PLATE.

The view is taken from the most eligible part of an opposite field. The centre door is the entrance to the boxes only. The avenue to the pit and gallery is in the obscured side of the projection. The house adjoining the theatre, (on the left of the spectator), was erected by Mr. ROBSON, from whom it became the property of Mr. KING, and is at present occupied by Mr. C. LE BAS, Master of the Ceremonies. The back parlour, opposite the Shakspeare Tavern, (which just appears), is rented separately as a box-office, treasury, &c. under the direction of Mr. DALE, who succeeded his father, (a man of great respectability), in a similar situation at Drury-Lane. *At the end of the building, on the perspective side, is the stage door, standing in* Prince's-Street, *partly hidden by the head of a female figure. The box-office is admirably situated, contiguous to* Hawley-Square. *The circular aperture in front is intended to ventilate the gallery; and the windows on each side the entrance are deceptions only.*

D 2   THEATRE,

THEATRE, TUNBRIDGE-WELLS.

THE earliest information we have been able to collect concerning the theatricals of this place of fashionable resort, mentions only, that an itinerant group exhibited their drolls, in 1737; since which a man, known by the name of *Canterbury* SMITH, bestowed occasional visits, and was succeeded by a performer of his company, of the name of PETERS, in 1753, who used a room belonging to a public-house not far from the situation of the present theatre. Mrs. BAKER, whom we have already introduced to public notice, has played here about thirty years. She erected a temple to the muses on *Mount Sion*, but a small distance from the place where Mr. CUMBERLAND, the author, now resides. She used this building but two seasons, during both of which, she was strenuously attacked by a company under the management of Mr. GLASSINGTON, in a place now distinguished as HUNT's Warehouse, both playing on the same evening, in a true spirit of opposition; but Mrs. BAKER proving the more successful general, the conquered party listed under the banners of the Amazonian victor. At the request of several of her friends, the theatre was demolished, and a new one erected, partly with the old materials, on the scite of some premises adjoining the Sussex Tavern, securing it by lease. Here she remained unmolested, till the building falling into want of repair, she formed a resolution of pulling it down, to substitute a new one on an extensive and more elegant scale. This work was begun in the latter end of the year 1801, and finished so as to be performed in, on the 8th of July, 1802. Prices, boxes 4s. pit 2s. and gallery 1s. Upper boxes, or slips, the same as the pit. It is neat, with a dwelling house in front—cost from fifteen to sixteen hundred pounds, and holds about sixty. This edifice is rendered remarkable, by standing in different counties, *Sussex* receiving the stage, and *Kent* the auditory: the sewer dividing the one from the other, running underneath the orchestra; a circumstance peculiarly *fortunate* for the members of the sock and buskin in a migrating company, as they may easily evade the hand of justice, by *stepping* into another jurisdiction. There is only one pay place, which Mrs. BAKER *always* occupies. The dressing rooms, which are underneath the stage, are

bad;

TUNBRIDGE WELLS.

London, Published 1st April 1804, William St. Strand.

bad; and the green room, the actor's luxury, is to be erected, when Mrs. Manager shall think one necessary. Mr. CUMBERLAND usually superintends the getting up of his own pieces at this theatre; and here, first discovered the merit of Mr. DOWTON, (Mrs. BAKER's son-in-law), who has since so amply justified his recommendation on the boards of *Drury-Lane*. There are only two things necessary to render *Tunbridge Wells* an excellent theatre—good actors and good scenery: though, to confess the truth, the *decorations* are but scanty. Performers enjoy only a third of their benefit nights receipts, the remainder being stopped to defray expences. The success of this place, and consequently of the theatre, is wholly dependant on its visitors, which are numerous and fashionable; but charges of all descriptions, particularly at the inns, are so exorbitant, that those only who possess the advantage of *plenty* must expect to enjoy a respectable accommodation. Mr. and Mrs. BAKER were, some thirty years ago, performers in the company of Mrs. WAKELIN, (the latter's mother), about which time the former died. Mrs. BAKER then attended fairs, with rope-dancing, pantomime, burletta, &c. &c. till accumulating some cash at *Gosport*, she struck out into the regular drama.

DESCRIPTION OF THE PLATE.

The view is taken from the Walks, or, what are more generally termed the Pantiles, which are raised some feet above the Theatre itself, as the figure demonstrates, who is seen in the act of ascending from the latter to the former, discovering thereby, the communication from one to the other.

THEATRE,

THEATRE, READING

READING Theatricals, as far as our information extends, originated with the grammar school plays of Doctor VALPY, whose boys performed on Wednesday the 7th of October, 1755, before the Vice Chancellor of *Oxford*. Previous to the year 1788, the *public* drama met but small encouragement, in consequence of the great irregularities of one JOHNSON's Company " whose conduct was so bad," to quote from the authority before us, " The women being all———; and the men all rogues." The impression made by these persons, was, as must naturally be imagined, of so strong and so disgusting a nature, that a Mr. SMITH, and MARK MOORE, alias Signor MORINI, of rambling and eccentric memory, who seperately reared their motley standard, were obliged to " fret their hour" in a barn in the *outskirts* of the town, from a resolution of the Magistrates never again to suffer vagrants to exercise their calling *in* it. This impression, however, though strong, it seems was not indelible ; for, in 1788, THORNTON had the address to gain an abrogation of the dreadful edict, and to obtain permission to erect a Theatre. He constantly attends the races, and after reaping the golden profits of a two months harvest, retires, like the Sun, to gild a new horizon. This edifice, situate in *Friar-street*, has one general entrance, and money-taker, to boxes, pit and gallery; which is the only explanation that the *plate* seems capable of admitting. We cannot compliment the scenery, the decorations, nor the attendance in the orchestra. As far as the pay-place, the passage is good and roomy ; but, afterwards, particularly that part of it branching to the pit, is very bad. The house will hold upwards of forty pounds. Boxes 3*s.* pit 2*s.* and gallery 1*s.* half price, or any price is taken. THORNTON first displayed his theatrical abilities (which he continues to exercise with as much effect as ever) under Mr. WHEELER's management at *Portsmouth* (who brought him from *Plymouth* as his prompter), by performing characters, in case of illness, without studying, or *reading*, them---it was sufficient to explain to him the nature of the part, and his soaring genius, with the assistance of some speeches from a favorite play (for every actor has his darling piece) brought him off with laurels. He has lately found it *necessary* to procure a partner.

THEATRE,

READING.

London, Publish'd 1. April 1804, by I Woodhill, Villiers S. Strand.

THEATRE.

BRIGHTON.

London, Publish'd 1.April, 1804, by T.Wentfield. Wilton S.t Strand.

THEATRE, BRIGHTON.

THE Theatrical History of this place is quite of a modern date, *Brighton* having been, (till of late years, it received the stamp of fashion,) a poor fishing town, visited only by strollers and village hunters—a class of people travelling from spot to spot, staying a single night at each. Their theatre is composed of canvass, strained upon hoisted poles, which, when taken down is easily portable by hand. No regular establishment appears till the year 1774, when Mr. SAMUEL PAINE, bricklayer of *Brighton*, built a theatre in *North-Street*, which is still standing, but converted into a printing-office, wine-vaults, &c. &c. (*Vide Plate in a subsequent Number*) ; and which he let to Mr. ROGER JOHNSON, for the term of three years. The House was then disposed of by lease to the late Mr. Fox, tavern-keeper of *Bow-Street*, *Covent-Garden*, for fifteen years, at sixty guineas per year : Mr. PAINE covenanting for an annual benefit, free of expence, and free admission for himself and family on all occasions. Notwithstanding this agreement, a variety of disputes occurred between the landlord and his tenant, for the first two years, concerning the former part of it ; Mr. Fox sending a bill of charges, because the writings, through the neglect or the design of the person employed to draw them, did not categorically state that the incidental expences of the benefit were to be allowed, as well as the benefit itself. Mr. PAINE, in revenge for this injustice, singularly availed himself of his second prerogative, (which did not admit the like demur), by regularly collecting on every representation his children and relations to take possession of the best and the most fashionable seats, to the great disadvantage of the manager, and the total exclusion of all other applicants. They at length, resorted to arbitration to adjust the difference, which was effected by a decision, that Mr. PAINE should pay the half only of the charges, which were twenty pounds, by way of compromise. In 1790, about two years previous to the expiration of the lease, Fox erected the present theatre, in *Duke-Street* ; and as the licence which gave legality to the performances, was annually granted by the magistrates of *Lewes*, in his name, he met with no opposition in transferring his operations from the one to the other. Mr. Fox did not enjoy the fruit of his labours, dying shortly after, involved to the amount of about £.2700. The creditors resolved to sell the property; and Mr. COBB, an attorney of

Clement's.

Clement's-Inn, being on a summer's excursion to the Races, with a friend, in 1793, was prevailed on by the latter, who had some knowledge of the widow, to use his endeavours to procure a purchaser, (Mrs. Fox expecting thereby not only to pay the debts, but secure a surplus, with some theatrical privileges to herself), Mr. COBB was unable to succeed, on account of the incumbrances connected with the purchase, viz. a free benefit and annuity to Mrs. Fox, and great uncertainty of the renewal of the licénce, as Mr. PAINE was applying for a requalification for the former theatre. However, having taken an interest in the affair, through Miss NELLY FOX, (now Mrs. BROWN), who earnestly supported her mother's entreaties for relief and assistance; notwithstanding he was ill qualified for such a business, scarcely ever entering a Theatre in London, " Stabbed by a white wench's black eye," consented to advance the sum of £1,600, by way of mortgage. The creditors having agreed to take a composition : in *December* following, he brought the amount in a post chaise, to the castle tavern, and satisfied the several claimants according to the nature of their demands,—bond debts, sixteen shillings, others, fourteen, in the pound. In *April*, 1794, Mr. PAINE applied at *Lewes* for the licence, not having acceded to Mr. Fox's offer of £100 to relinquish his pretensions, on the building of the present Theatre. The matter was referred to arbitration, and decided that Mr. COBB should pay him £130 and his expences, amounting in the whole to £150 ; after which, COBB naturally thought himself secure of his licence ; but our Readers will see in the account of *Lewes*, that he had other difficulties to encounter. The next year, he allowed the widow £100, besides the benefit; and engaged Mr. POWELL, of *Covent Garden* (since dead) to manage under him ; but, finding at the close of the Season, that he had lost near £200, he declined in future, any concern in the active part, previously making some necessary arrangements, and allowing the widow seventy pounds by way of annuity. When Mrs. Fox died, the benefit was continued to her daughter, before-mentioned, who, on her marriage, dropped it ; and the annuity was divided between herself, her sister, and her brother ; the last of whom, returning from abroad, disposed of his share to Mr. COBB, who soon after purchased the others also, whereby the whole concern became his property. The ground on which the Theatre is erected, is the property of a minor, who will become of age in about three years, and is subject to a rent of twenty guineas, on a lease that expires about the year 1810. The Princess of WALES visiting *Brighton in* 1796, frequented the theatre so much as to occasion the proprietor to expend nearly £.600, in converting the internal square form into that of a horse-shoe.

The

The idea that the royal visit would be annually repeated, however, proved fallacious, for she never afterwards appeared there. Some years prior to this, a singular coincidence took place; the Prince of WALES, and the Duke and Duchess of GLOUCESTER, *seperately* bespoke a play and farce, which proved to be for each night " The Chapter of Accidents," and " The Agreeable Surprize"—Jacob and Lingo by TOM BAKER—Bridget and Cowslip by Mrs. WILSON. After the decease of Mr. Fox, the Theatre was conducted by the late Mr. JOHN PALMER, of *Drury-Lane*, in the summers of 1792 and 1793, assisted in the latter by Mr. WILD; Mr. PALMER having his *Hay-market* business to attend to, which occasioned his performing alternately at both houses throughout the season—an instance of professional industry which we believe has never been exceeded, if we except Mr. ELLISTON's alternate exhibitions at *Bath* and *London*, that procured him the title of the Telegraphic Actor: Mr. PALMER was to have reigned for two years longer, but he neglected to fulfil his engagement. In 1795, the Theatre was let to BERNARD, and the three following seasons to DIDDEAR. 1799, 1800, and 1801, were confirmed by lease to Messrs. BLOGG and ARCHER; but, after the second season, in consequence of a difference, ARCHER seceded, and SWENDALL was appointed to the management for the remainder of the term. 1802 and 1803 were governed by Mr. HAYMES. With such a manager and such a company, little entertainment to the public, or profit to himself could reasonably be expected: he was indebted to Mr. BRAHAM for almost the only success that he experienced. We read in the " Monthly Mirror," (the best periodical work of the kind now published), the following just observation respecting this person: " From some domestic concern or other, the manager is perpetually bringing out women of loose character." The Thespian Dictionary informs us, that he is a native of *Devonshire*, and was intended for the occupation of a wheelwright, for which calling Nature seems evidently to have designed him. Persons curious to know more concerning him, may be gratified by a reference to the last mentioned authority. The prices of admission till within these two years were, Boxes 4s. Pit 2s. and Gallery 1s. The Boxes and Pit are now advanced to 5s. and 2s. 6d. and the charges from twenty, to eight and twenty pounds. The House will hold at these encreased terms, from £.100 to £.110, when *quite full*:—no half price is taken. The advance of rent has doubtless been the occasion of the increase of price; Mr. COBB having gradually raised it from £.200 to £.450 per annum; paying all outgoings; and charging for each of the last two years, no less than £.500, clear and unencumbered. The Theatre is supposed to have cost about £.2,500; and the

E   licence

licence is annually renewed at *Lewes*, for the trifling sum of three guineas. When the tax on hair powder first came up, it was exceedingly unpopular at *Brighton*, insomuch that persons using it, subjected themselves to public insult; Mr. Fox, the late manager's son, having a character to perform, which rendered powder necessary, applied it to one side of his head, and not the other, (reminding us of the figure, one half of which is pourtrayed as a skeleton, and the other as a beau); being interrogated as to the reason of the oddity, he replied, that he did it to please both parties. It is with much pleasure we announce, that a gentleman, of great experience in the dramatic world, has undertaken the management for the ensuing season. We trust that with such a commander as Mr. BRUNTON, it will prove a prosperous campaign—though *Brighton* is certainly a bad theatrical town, having a *London* audience for the most part to perform to, who retire thither, not to see what they have so repeatedly witnessed the preceding winter, in superior style; but to enjoy the salubrious qualities of sea breezes, bathing, the fashionable promenades, &c.

DESCRIPTION OF THE PLATE.

The Door under the portico is the general entrance to the Boxes, and particularly used for carriages: the door on the dark side of it is in imitation of a real one, immediately opposite, which is also an entrance to the Boxes. The way to the Pit and Gallery is through the folding doors in the circular wall, seen in the engraving: that to the Stage door, through a similar aperture directly opposite. The whole of the front is of wood.

THEATRE-

GALLERY PIT BOXES

R I C H M O N D .

London, Publish'd Feb.ʸ 1, 1804, by T Woodfall, Villers S.ᵗ Strand.

THEATRE-ROYAL, RICHMOND.

RICHMOND, or, as it was formerly denominated, *Sheen*, had a Theatre in 1730, or before; as, about that period, the famous PINKETHMAN, of facetious memory, burlesqued the tragedy of Cato in it: ADDISON, happily for his feelings, being dead. Himself and NORRIS represented Juba and the Roman Hero; the female characters were sustained by men; and none but low comedians were suffered to be concerned. The reader, who may wish for a specimen of the language adopted on this occasion, will find his curiosity gratified by referring to page 66 of the third volume of the Thespian Magazine, where this occurrence is registered, but not the scene of it. Some person, disgusted with the misapplied buffoonery, in the morning posted on the door the following lines:

> " While greatness hears such language spoke,
> " Where godlike Freedom's made a joke;
> " Let such mean souls be never free
> " To taste the sweets of Liberty."

A Theatre was built on the *Hill*, by CHAPMAN, an actor on the *London* boards, (to whom NED SHUTER was errand boy), somewhere about 1733; but dying ten or twelve years afterwards, the House experienced a number of vicissitudes, being let to puppet-shows, exhibitions, methodist declaimers, &c. &c. In 1748, died THOMSON, the noted author of the " Seasons;" who was buried at the west end of the north aisle of *Richmond* church. He lived in *Ross Dale House*, now, or lately Mrs. BOSCAWEN's residence, in the garden of which is still preserved the poet's favourite seat. SHUTER had *Richmond* in 1756, from whence Mr. LACY engaged Miss BARTON, (the present Mrs. ABINGTON). In 1762, the Theatre was under the management of Messrs. BURTON and BRANSBY. The company continued to play for a short time after the opening of the New Theatre; but not perceiving it to answer, they sold the property, part of which was purchased by Mr. LOVE, son of DANCE, the city architect, whose memory will never be erased, while his clumsy and ill-

contrived

contrived design, the *Mansion-House*, exists to blazon it. Mr. DANCE assumed
the name of LOVE, on commencing a theatrical life. He played in *London*,
but was by no means a general performer, being liked but, in few characters,
though in those few he evidently excelled: his Falstaff for instance, was, in
those days, unequalled. The present House was begun about the latter end
of the year 1764, and opened in May, 1765, by the said Mr. LOVE. It is
erected on the scite of an old mansion, which was divided, and let out in
tenements, and afterwards bought by Mr, HORNE and Colonel HUBBALD his
son-in-law, of Mr. PUGH, watchmaker at *Brentford*. A bricklayer of *Richmond*, of the name of ALDER, who still resides there, completed the edifice
from a model of *Old Drury*, under the direction of Mr. BUTLER, architect and
principal machinist of that Theatre. We do not envy Mr. BUTLER his task
of superintending a man, whose ideas never extended beyond brick and
mortar. The scenery was executed by Mr. WILLIAMS, now, or lately,
painter to the Theatre, *York*. At this time was standing the hamlet of *West
Sheen*, (consisting of eighteen houses, and the old priory gate), which, in 1770,
was totally annihilated, and the ground added to his Majesty's inclosures.
Mr. LOVE was succeeded in 1773, by BOOTH and KENNEDY ; the latter of
whom was an useful actor, and an honest, but most unfortunate man. His
wife lost her life in the dreadful fire in *King-Street*, *Covent-Garden*, with
CATHERINE, a relation of Mr. YOUNGER, whose unhappy end is recorded on
a grave-stone, in the north side of the church-yard. Mr. KENNEDY's face
was so much burned in endeavouring to extricate his wretched partner, that
he found it a material drawback in his profession : in short, on the death of his
friend and patron, Mr. HENDERSON, he sunk into perfect indigence, and put
to a miserable existence, a more miserable period, by the application of a
razor, in July, 1786, in the sixty-sixth year of his age. In 1774, the well
known veteran JEFFERSON, who now resides at *Plymouth*, and of whom we
shall have much to say, when we mention that Theatre, in conjunction with
SLINGSBY, took the Theatre on lease, but at the close of the third season, at
the request of the proprietors, (who wished to dispose of their property), they
relinquished their claim. At this time the Theatre was put up for sale, and
knocked down by SKINNER, for £.3610, to Mr. WALDRON, who forfeited the
deposit, and the property reverted to the proprietor. Mr. HORNE at his
decease, bequeathed his share to Colonel HUBBALD's three children—Mrs.
CURRIE ; a daughter since dead ; and a son who lives in obscurity, afflicted
with a dreadful malady.

In

In 1777 and 1778. Mr. WHEBLE, a tallow-chandler of *Richmond*, and another, rented the concern. In 1779 and 1780, WALDRON and Co. succeeded. Half price was attempted, without success, the former year, and has since been discontinued. In 1781 and 1782, the Theatre was rented by twelve tradesmen, called by the town's-folk, (though we confess ourselves at a loss for the affinity), the Twelve Apostles. Mr. WILLIAM PALMER rented it 1783, 1784, and 1785. In 1786, 1787, and 1788, the Theatre was conducted by Mr. STEVENS, in whose first or second season, died the celebrated actress, Mrs. HAMILTON, whose distresses first suggested the idea of a theatrical fund, though they were never succoured by its fostering influence. Mrs. JORDAN first played here in 1789, under the management of Mr. WYNNE, who held the Theatre that and the following year. Miss BARNES performing Wilhelmina, in the Waterman, not having learned the second act, found it necessary (to prevent the odium of incorrectness from attaching to her study), to excite the commisseration of the audience, by fainting on the stage. The stratagem would infallibly have answered, had she not exposed the trick, by telling the carpenter, who ran on to her assistance, *to be careful of her gown*, before he had borne her out of sight and hearing. WYNNE was an excellent pantomimic actor ; he never publicly performed, but instructed those who did. He was a man easily discomposed, and easily restored. A sudden occurrence once induced him to post a bill on the Theatre, purporting that it had closed. Mr. PARSONS, who managed under him, was absent on a short aquatic excursion with some of the performers, and, at his return, remonstrated on the impropriety of this proceeding ; whereupon the notice was immediately withdrawn, and the season suffered to proceed. Mr. PARSONS left there a scene of his own painting, representing *Richmond Bridge*. On the 11th of August, 1790, Lord BARRYMORE performed the part of Scaramouch, in Don Juan, for Mr. EDWIN's benefit; and Mr. HARRY ANGELO, the greasy heroine of the Minor. The female part of WYNNE's company played for Lord BARRYMORE, at his Theatre, afterwards the *Fantoccini, Saville-Row*. In 1791, the concern fell into the hands of Messrs. BENSON, THOMPSON, and MACREADY ; and in the four following years to Mr. WATHEN. This gentleman, (the son of Dr. WATHEN), was bred to the profession of arms, and promoted to a lieutenancy in the 39th regiment, at the memorable Siege of *Gibraltar*. Having joined in some private theatricals abroad, he assisted in those of Lord BARRYMORE at his return ; and after playing at several country theatres, under his christian name of GEORGE, he joined the standard of *Drury-Lane*, from which profitable scene of action he has lately made an honorable retreat, and taken up

his

his head quarters, as barrack-master, at *Steyning.* His *rencontre* in the first year of his management, with JOHN WILLIAMS, better known by the title of *Anthony Pasquin*, is too notorious to need, and too prolix to bear insertion. Mr. WILLIAMES, (*not Pasquin*), who succeeded Mr. Fox, in the Tavern, *Bow-Street*, was the Captain's deputy, and getting up a pantomime for his benefit, procured an elephant from *Sadler's-Wells*, which he was necessitated to take to pieces; it being otherwise too bulky for admission. At a benefit granted this year to one LEWIS, an old inhabitant, (the whole of the Pit being laid into the Boxes, and the Gallery admission doubled), the House produced above a hundred pounds. When the Younger COLMAN succeeded to the *Hay-Market*, in 1795, he instituted a legal process against our manager, for pirating, as he thought, the Farce of The Agreeable Surprize. The verdict of a jury has, however, established, that no copy-right bears sufficient authority to prevent a representation out of the metropolis. In 1796, the government of the Theatre became quadripartite under HAYMES, mentioned in the last account; FOLLETT, the noted clown; CROSS, the composer of ballet pantomimes, at the *Royal Circus*; and REES, the imitator. The following season was under HAYMES alone, who also fitted up a barn at *Hampton Wick*, where the Stadtholder honored him with many a somnolent nod. What with fancy dresses, and ladies' first appearances, he made the Theatre to answer, this and the summer of 1798; though it could not boast of particular estimation. In this year died the proprietor, Colonel HUBBALD.

In 1799, the House was rented by a gentleman, who assumed the name of NEVILLE. His inexperience in theatrical affairs submitted him to a variety of impositions. Blue-Beard, and that *maker* of managers, PIZARRO, got up at a great and unnecessary expence, (upwards of £.200; uncommon for the country), made some amends at the end of the season, for the losses and disappointments of a bad commencement. The original intention of this season was, to bring forward a set of actors, whose merits had been tried, and generally approved of, at the Private Theatre, in *Tottenham-Court-Road*, a place at that time, of great consequence in dramatic estimation, but now sunk almost into oblivion. How far the attempt succeeded, may be seen by the following persons, whom this adventure has brought upon the stage:— Mr. FAULKNER and Mrs. BASTER, now at *Edinburgh*; Mr. NOBLE, at *Newcastle*, who is engaged at the *Hay-Market* the ensuing season; Mr. JONES, at *Dublin*; Mr. LOVEGROVE, *Bath*; Miss DAVIS, at the *Hay-Market*, &c. &c. When the Comedy of Sighs was brought forward at this Theatre, Mrs.

BASTER

BASTER, who played Josephine, repeated from similar motives, the experiment of Miss BARNES, as recently mentioned, but with more success, and with this addition :—Wheu recovered, Mr. B. requested her not to faint again, *till she got home.*

The four seasons remaining to be accounted for, were under the direction of Mr. DIDDEAR, the manager of *Dover*, and Mr. COPELAND, groom to the late Mr. FECTOR, banker, and principal proprietor of the *Dover Theatre*, and formerly of superior eminence as a private actor. Our correspondent adds, that last year, the *Groom jockeyed* DIDDEAR out of the concern. Their plan being on a confined scale, and renting the Theatre a fourth year, seem to warrant us in concluding that the adventure has been successful. On the 22nd of October, 1802, Their MAJESTIES and the PRINCESSES honored the Theatre for the first time, with their royal presence—the performances were the Belle's Stratagem, and the Miser. In 1803, a kind of coalition took place, by admitting Messrs. POWELL and RUSSELL, (who are to hold the Theatre the ensuing summer). Having thus completed our plan of giving the several managers in their order of succession, there only remains to make a few observations on the Theatre itself. How it came to be distinguished by the epithet of Royal, otherwise than by courtesy from its vicinage to *Kew*, we are altogether unable to determine. The Prologue spoken on its opening, contains an express declaration that it was " by commission made a royal sloop." But with all due deference, we apprehend the assertion to be wrong; or how could they insert in the lease, a clause prohibiting performances without a licence previously obtained from the Chamberlain's Office. Indeed, the Theatrical Biography, published in 1772, expresses that Mr. LOVE obtained a *patent ;* which, if true, must have long since expired, aud consequently the title it conveys; but " Once a Captain,"—" The proverb is somewhat musty"—the Royal Visits may now be said to have renewed the right, and therefore we dismiss the subject. PETER CURRIE, Esq. a Captain in the East Middlesex Militia, succeeded Colonel HUBBALD as proprietor, in right of his wife, the Colonel's daughter, both names appearing in the deeds. Internally considered, we may pronounce this House a model for theatrical architects. Before the curtain are commodious Boxes, and a roomy Pit, with every convenience. Behind it are twenty-four feet depth of stage, terminated by an arch, beyond which the stage may occasionally be lengthened twenty feet. Having exceeded our limits for a single theatre, we are under the necessity of briefly stating, that there is no convenience or accommodation which

may

may not be found.   One thing, however, it would be an injustice to our readers to pass so slightly over—we mean, the great facility which with the Theatre may be converted into an elegant ball-room, that has served as a pattern for many others.   The Pit and Stage are completely furnished with a temporary flooring; the fronts of the Boxes taken down; by which means their seats appear but as so many benches to surround the room : the entrance is from the centre Box.   The wings being removed, a complete frame work, painted by a capital artist, reduces the sides of the Stage to a level with the Boxes.   A tremendous piece of machinery forms a ceiling of one entire mass ; and being on play nights suspended by ropes, that have borne the wearing tug of many a year, it is naturally become the terror of the actor. An inclosure of the front seats of the Gallery forms an excellent orchestra.   The Stage doors serve as avenues to places of refection, which are well laid out, and every way appropriate.   Through the arch (before mentioned), is a capacious card room,   Two handsome glass chandeliers are suspended.   In short, the whole is so complete, and the metamorphose accomplished in so short a time, that any stranger who witnessed a performance on the Monday evening, would scarcely credit that the Tuesday's ball was conducted in the self same area.

That *Richmond*, generally speaking, is a bad 'theatrical resort, the great variety of its managers, we judge to sufficiently testify; there being no less than thirty-seven, in nine and thirty years.   As a further proof, in STEVENS's time, PARSONS, BANNISTER. jun. and PALMER, played in Who's the Dupe ? to eleven pounds.   For this, some reasons may be assigned :—the number of beautiful and rural walks; its vicinity to *London*; fashionable tea and card parties, and not always the best actors.   The premises, which are copyhold of the manor of *Richmond*, cost about £.8.000.   The season is generally from June to October.   The original rent was £.250 per annum, at which it continued many years ; then gradually dwindled to £.100, though it has lately risen to £.130 ; near six pounds the licence ; and a wardrobe keeper entailed by the proprietor, at a weekly stipend of fifteen shillings.   During Mr. LOVE's management, the Pit was 2s. 6d. since that period 2s. Boxes always 4s. and Gallery 1s.   Queen ELIZABETH was confined here, during the reign of her sister, for a short time, in the very place which was afterwards her favorite residence : the gate, or entrance, is now standing, in the rentage of Mr. DUNDAS.   We shall conclude our account with a few lines from GARRICK's opening prologue, before alluded to :

                                                            The

" The ship now launch'd, with necessaries stor'd,
" Rigg'd, mann'd, well-built, and a right freight on board;
" All ready, tight and trim, from head to poop,
" And, by *commission*, made a *royal sloop :*
" May heaven from tempests, rocks, and privateers
" Preserve the *Richmond*—give her, boys, three cheers !"

DESCRIPTION OF THE PLATE.

The Tree is preserved in the engraving, for its antiquity, as well as its picturesque appearance, having been planted by the hand of the Maiden Queen, and thereby, as memorable as SHAKSPEARE'S *Mulberry. The several entrances are pointed out by the writing underneath the portico. The front is certainly mean; and having to gain the Pit by a descent of several steps, it is not only extremely dangerous on crowded nights, (the melancholy instance at the* Hay-Market *some years since, affording an example), but furnishes a receptacle in wet weather for mud and filth. The ascent to the Gallery door was formerly so unsafe, that several persons were much hurt by being pushed over the hand-rail that alone protected it, on the night of Lord* BARRYMORE'S *performance. The window over the Box door is only a deception; that over the Gallery, lights the stairs thereof; the centre large one belongs to the Box lobby; and the circular ditto, to the Gallery. There is one Stage door behind the building, and another at the right hand side of it. The bow windowed-house is usually the habitation of the manager, being included in the lease; and contains in one corner of the kitchen, a private communication with the Pit passage, from whence there is a door leading beneath the Stage. This is said to have been the contrivance of, and to have been found extremely* convenient *by a former manager. Immediately behind the House is a range of buildings, that contains the dressing-rooms, &c. and which is partly discovered.*

F

THEATRE,

THEATRE, NEWBURY.

LIKE most of THORNTON's theatrical towns, were we to trace the drama in this place, it would only be to enumerate a catalogue of strolling companies of the most inferior order. It will suffice to say, that the present Theatre was finished in the month of November, 1802, by Mr. THORNTON, who had performed for several years in a temporary building. Notwithstanding the title it assumes, the House is situate in the *Spene*, or *Speenham Land*, on the river *Kennet*; as the magistrates of *Newbury* refused a licence within their jurisdiction. The Theatre forms one side of a sort of square, built on some waste ground, formerly terminated by a wall. It is a small House, but neatly fitted up—the Boxes are lined with crimson damask: the centre Box is private, and is decorated for the reception of the Margravine of ANSPACH, who occasionally distinguishes it with her presence, when at her neighbouring seat at *Benham*, where she has also a Theatre of her own; a draught of which will, by her kind permission, grace an ensuing number. Her Serene Highness generously afforded her patronage to the benefits of the first season. The audience are admitted by one general entrance.

Mr. THORNTON is so remarkable for absence of mind, that he has frequently gone to *London* from *Windsor*, to purchase some article wanted for the Theatre, and returned without it; indeed, as a further proof, it is recorded of him, when dressing for an evening's performance, he sought, where it was usually deposited, preparatory to his dressing, for a clean shirt, and not finding it, sent to Mrs. THORNTON, who assured him she had put four there the day previous; however, as not one could be found, another was again sent for, and brought him; when preparing to proceed in accoutreing himself, it was discovered he had already put on the four, in the search for which so much time had been lost.

The

NEWBURY.

London, Published Nov.r 1, 1804 by Ackerman, Filler.s S.t Strand

The only time that THORNTON ever played in *London,* was on a bye night at the *Hay-Market Theatre,* for the benefit of Mr. EVERARD, an excellent low comedian, and a reputed son of GARRICK. The play was the Clandestine Marriage; the character of Mrs. Heidelberg by Mrs. GARDNER, being her first and only appearance on the Stage, after a seventeen years absence in the *West Indies.* As THORNTON was entering the Theatre, he received *a touch on the shoulder,* that produced a momentary consternation ; however, a timely *touch on the palm,* induced Mr, Deputy LATITAT to wait the conclusion of the piece, in which our hero represented the antiquated debauchee with uncommon *eclat*; and, moreover, uncommon correctness ; afterwards submitting, with the utmost composure to the even handedness of justice.

DESCRIPTION OF THE PLATE.

The houses on both sides are inhabited by working people, also the two tenements whose entrances are underneath the portico. The center folding doors are the only communication with the Theatre; the arms in the pediment are painted proper; *those over the entrance are of composition; the pillars were transported from* St. John's College, Oxford; *and a dial is intended to occupy the circle in the upper pediment. The whole has certainly a more appropriate appearance than any other of* THORNTON'S *Theatres.*

THEATRE,

THEATRE, PORTSMOUTH.

W E introduce the theatrical history of this place, with observing, that as far back as 1732, Mr. MACKLIN performed here as a member of an itinerant company, since which period, there is little on record that appears decisive, till 1758, when Mr, KENNEDY, manager of the *Plymouth* and *Exeter* Theatres, visited *Portsmouth* in the summer, with a sharing company, (generally called the Brandy Company, from the intemperance of its members), where the following season, Mrs. OSBORNE, from *North America*, in the fifth act of the Mourning Bride, became a *joyful mother*. Mr. MOODY, who had just returned from *America* also, was, at this Theatre, engaged by Mr. GARRICK for *Drury-Lane*, where he soon afterwards appeared, in the character of King Henry the Eighth. Mr. VICTOR says, that he here witnessed the representation of Richard the Third, in which, on Richard's exclaiming—" Oh, take more pity in thine eyes, and see him here," Miss WHITE, in Lady Anne, indignantly replied—" Would they were *battle-axe* to strike *the dead*." At the close of the season in 1760, Mr. KENNEDY took away with him the scenery and the wings; on which ARTHUR, the manager of *Bath*, projected the building of another Theatre. The opening of this House, which was on the 20th of July, 1761, with Hamlet, and Contrivances, was attended with circumstances of a singular nature. The Theatre both within and without, exhibited such a rude, and unfinished state, there being not a single seat in the pit, and the stage waist deep in shavings, that, at twelve o'clock, the whole company pronounced it impossible to play. But where are the difficulties which may n ot be surmounted by extraordinary talents and determined will? The wonder-working ARTHUR completed all by seven; but the populace after three hours waiting in the street, eager to gain admission, and indulge their curiosity in a new house, new actors, and, (to them), a new play, had become, the sailors particularly, quite unruly; when suddenly the manager appeared among them, arrayed not like his advertised Polonius, but more resembling Hecate, or her witches. He was decorated with an old flapped hat, and woman's apron, grasping a broom, and peeping from a visage as black and

greasy

PORTSMOUTH.

London. Publish'd Nov.r 17. 1804. by I. Woodpall, Villier S.t Strand.

greasy as any barn Othello in the dog days. Thus accoutred, he harangued the multitude, humbly soliciting their patience, while the carpenters cleared the shavings from the pit and gallery—he then retired amidst the laughs and hootings of the mob; who, shortly after, on a given signal, burst through the doors, and overturned the orator and his broom together, which possessed no other charm than to assist him to hobble an escape with the little expedition left him. There being neither persons nor offices prepared for taking money the sailors and their lasses had only to arrange themselves agreeably to their fancy; nevertheless, ARTHUR proved himself a collected and collecting manager; for as soon as the house was filled, and all a little quiet, though seated in a cloud of dust, he took the circuit of the theatre, and gathered whatever he could muster either by threats or by civility. (Probably this circumstance operated as an example to Mr. ELLISTON, at his recent benefit, only Mr. E. *improved* upon the principle, as the idea of appointing receiving houses to relieve the conscientious of their debt, never once suggested itself to our chop-fallen manager.) Some paid, others were obstinate, and the rest contributed just what they pleased; however, nothing could induce our hero to quit the charge, while there remained a prospect of another shilling. In a few evenings they got to rights, and were well attended, as the theatre was evidently superior to that they were accustomed to, and which was now re-occupied by the *Plymouth* company, who maintained their opposition the following summer. It afterwards fell into the hands of Mr. SAMUEL JOHNSON, who after occupying it a single season, let it to Mr. MATTOCKS and Mr. SIMPSON, to whom in 1776 WHEELER became deputy. In 1785, the first symptoms of Mr. BRERETON's insanity discovered themselves at this theatre, in the part of Lovel in the Clandestine Marriage, when he obliged his wife, the present Mrs. KEMBLE, who personated Fanny, to dance a minuet, which is totally irrelavent to the character. In the last act of SHAKSPEARE's Posthumous, he came dancing on the stage, and altered a number of the speeches. He played Alexander the Great, for a benefit. In the scene where Statira says —— "Hold off, and let me rush into his arms," he turned short round, went off the stage, and left her to make the best of it. When she lay dead, he walked up to her, and exclaimed " O my poor dear little ——, who could have used you so?" About eighteen or nineteen years ago, a Mr. PERRY, an actor in WHEELER's company, having quarrelled with the manager, agreed with KENT, the landlord of the Goat public-house, to build an opposition theatre between the half-way houses and the gates; but, after all his exertions was unable to obtain a licence, in con-

G
sequence

sequence of which, the house was opened on the plan of *Sadler's Wells*. In a short time they ventured upon farces, till at last some *plays* were winked at. They had not continued open above six months, when PERRY died, and the concern was carried on a little while by CORNELYS, for Mr. KENT; then finally dropt, to the ruin of the latter, who afterwards became a guard to one of the stage coaches. Near PERRY's theatre there was a public house, kept by one COOMBS, the present property man of *Covent Garden*, where BRERE-TON, WILLIAMS, and STAUNTON in a fit of ebriety, one day pelted the carriage of the Magistrate (Sir JOHN CARR) as it passed along, and nearly broke the pannels, for which they were reduced to the necessity of a public apology! Mr. COLLINS succeeded to the management in 1787, who was joined by DAVIES, who died in 1797, leaving his share of the property to his children. It was here that Miss STREET, afterwards known by the successive names of DANCER, BARRY, and CRAWFORD, made her first appearance in the character of Monimia, as did Mrs. ABINGTON in the *old theatre*, in the farce of the Virgin Unmasked. Neither the external nor internal appearance of the house entitles it to much consideration; and as so much money has been made here in time of war, we think the public have a right to expect a share of the emoluments to be expended in embellishment. The company is truly respect-able, a sample of which may be seen on the boards of *Drury Lane*, in the manager's son. The circuit consists of *Portsmouth, Winchester, Southampton, Chichester* and *Newport.* It was once proposed to WHEELER, by Mr. HUGHES, that *Exeter, Plymouth Dock* and *Salisbury* should be added to the circuit, on a sharing system, an opportunity then occurring of procuring a lease of the latter; but the levelling principle, and consequently the plan, was rejected by the former, as derogatory to the superiority of his talents, though we know not with what propriety, as he never had more than a weekly salary of thirty shillings, when playing at *Drury Lane.* The established law of performing under licence, not more than sixty nights, and that within four months, has been rigorously en-forced during Mr. COLLIN's management. The theatre will hold eighty pounds—expences twenty guineas—season the winter—prices 3s. 2s. 1s.

DESCRIPTION OF THE PLATE.

THE entrance to the Boxes is in the Doric portico, and to the Pit and Gallery by the door on the left side of the house. The stage door is down some steps under the further window, over which are the dressing-rooms, green-room, &c. &c.

THEATRE,

GRANTHAM.

London, Published 1 Dec.r 1804, by I. Woodfall, Villiers S.t Strand.

THEATRE, GRANTHAM.

THE *Lincoln* circuit, of which *Grantham* is a part, was established by *Doctor* HERBERT, (so called from the vulgar practice of *dignifying* every dabbler in physic) who was bred a surgeon and apothecary about fifty years ago. He had three sons and one daughter—the second (DENNIS) was placed in the accompt-ing house of—— HOGG, Esq. at *Lynn* in *Norfolk*, and by his care and industry has himself become a merchant of some consequence in *Bedfordshire*. His youngest son held an office in the *Lynn* customs ; and NATHANIEL the eldest, who is the only one that claims from us particular attention, was apprenticed to a butcher. When he arrived at years of maturity, he embarked as a per-former with a company of comedians to the *West Indies*, where he continued till the death of his father, when he returned to *England*, with a view of taking on himself the management of the vacant company, being not only the eldest son, but the only one on the stage. His mother, to whom the company was left, had resigned it to the memorable GEORGE ALEXANDER STEVENS, who had married her daughter, but finding his *Lecture on Heads* more profit-able, he had assigned the management to Mr. DYER, one of his principal per-formers, while he made his tour. Mr. HERBERT thus disappointed, meditated revenge, by endeavouring to form an opposition company, but in this he was equally unsuccessfull ;—at last, by the interference of their friends, his mother made over to him the property and management, for a stipulated sum and yearly income. To raise the means, he admitted Mr. JAMES AUGUSTUS WHITELY, of well-known theatrical memory, as a partner, being a monied man ; but he having another circuit to attend to, appointed Mr. JAMES SHAFTOE ROBINSON, father to the present manager, his deputy, who, after some time, purchased Mr. WHITELY's share. Mr. R. was born at *Ludlow*, *Shropshire*, and educated at the grammar-school, from which he absconded at the age of seventeen, and became an actor. In this situation he encountered the many vicissitudes attendant on the profession of the histrionic art. Travelling between the towns, in company with Mr. BENSLEY, lately of

Drury-

Drury-Lane, he found their *united stock* amount to a *single penny* ; with this they agreed to toss up for the purchase of a mutton pie, for the benefit of the happy winner.   Mr. R.. proving successful, BENSLEY, during the other's luscious banquet, stamped and swore like a truly hungry and irritated son of Thespis.   On another journey with Mr. HENRY KING, they suffered almost a three days abstinence ; at last they hit on the expedient of cutting off their hair, at that time worn long, and selling it to supply the common calls of hunger ; but the operation having nearly left them bald, they were under the necessity of refunding part of the produce for a couple of cherry-tree wigs, vulgarly so called, which they wore to the no small entertainment of their brethren.   Early in life he married Miss ANN FOWLER, of *Loughborough*, while in a company at that place.   He was afterwards engaged at *York*, under the successive management of ACHURCH and TATE WILKINSON, where he continued, till invited by WHITELY to superintend the *Lincoln* circuit.   He died at *Sheffield*.   Here we are in justice bound to contradict what the late Mr. WILKINSON says in his " *Wandering Patentee*," that Mr. J. S. ROBINSON was buried by a subscription of Free-Masons.   The Masons, from the respect they bore him, undoubtedly attended at his funeral ; but nothing more—he wanted no such aid, and the assertion must be painful to the feelings of his relatives ; though we are willing to believe that Mr. W. thought he had grounds for what he had stated.   Besides the present manager, he had issue, JAMES, part manager of the *Derby* and *Nottingham* circuit ; and GEORGE, a printer and stationer at *Peterborough*.   To return : after some years, HERBERT and ROBINSON contracted a partnership with Messrs. YOUNGER and MATTOCKS, in the management of *Manchester*, *Sheffield* and *Old Birmingham* Theatres, still retaining the *Lincoln* circuit.   This partnership not succeeding, they soon resigned it, and confined themselves to their usual *routine*, taking in a third partner, Mr. GREEN, who had been an officer promoted from the ranks.   In consequence of Mr. ROBINSON'S death, a twelvemonth after ; who was the active manager, and of allowed abilities both on the stage and off, the reputation of the company soon declined, together with its consequence, success and emolument.   Mr. GREEN purchased the vacant third for three hundred pounds ; and Mr HERBERT about three years afterwards, a little embarrassed in his private affairs, and tired of a falling scheme, by the advice of his brother DENNIS, sold his share to Mr. WHITFIELD, late of *Covent-Garden*, for a similar sum, when he took the White Horse Inn, at *Baldock*, where he died.   His reputation as a country actor, was very good, particularly in coarse comic cha-

racters,

racters, clowns in pantomimes, &c. &c. When a child, and just able to speak sufficiently for the stage, he represented the Duke of York, in the tragedy of King Richard the Third. When he should have said,—" O mother ! mother !" he made a pause ; the lady who performed the Queen, gave him the sentence several times, to which he at last replied—" You're not *my* mother ; give me my leather breeches, I want to go *hoame*." During a pantomime at *Sheffield*, in which he performed his favorite part of Clown, Harlequin disguised as a watchman, at the door of a night cellar, which opened by a trap, stood with his staff ready to strike him on the head when he appeared, for which purpose a wooden head was customarily provided. Unluckily at the moment, the block was missing ; when HERBERT, in the bustle, zealous for the cause, and thoughtless of the danger, used his own, which was instantly accosted with so severe a blow, that he fell back through the stage. A momentary consternation prevailed, in the idea that he was inevitably killed ; but their fears were soon subsided by hearing him bawl out in his Stentorian voice, " I'm a dead man ! he's killed me, he's killed me," and running directly on the stage, went through the character with his accustomed pleasantry. By his secession the firm became (the widow) ROBINSON, GREEN and WHITFIELD. WHITFIELD's *London* engagement compelled him to depute GREEN, whose sister he had married, to attend to his share of the concern ; but he being no actor, and unacquainted with theatrical matters, the company still more and more declined ; therefore seeing the necessity of making something of it while he could, he sold his share to Mr. MILLER, one of his actors, who two or three years before did not possess a single guinea, for, it is said, only one hundred and fifty pounds. A year or two after this, he purchased also WHITFIELD's share for less than one hundred pounds. THOMAS SHAFTOE, the eldest son of Mrs. ROBINSON, having become of age, she assigned her share to him. Thus they continued several years, when frequent dissentions rendered it adviseable to separate, and MILLER sold his shares to his competitor for twelve hundred pounds, who afterwards disposed of half the whole to Mr. ROBERT HENRY FRANKLIN, for nine hundred pounds. Mr. F. (of whom an account hereafter) remained five years, when he paid the debt of nature, leaving the property in trust for his only son. This partnership was as noted for unanimity, as the other for the contrary. Mr. R. married Miss Ross, sister-in-law to Mr. BRUNTON of *Covent Garden*, and daughter to the celebrated actress, Mrs. BROWN, formerly of the same theatre, whose style of acting, Mrs. JORDAN is said to have taken for her model. Mrs. ROBINSON is a considerable acquisition to the company, and would, no doubt,

have

have been on the *London* boards, but that her husband too well appreciates her value to his circuit. This is the gentleman whom we noticed on a wrapper, as styled by the Committee at Lloyd's the *Patriotic Manager*; he having first augmented the Patriotic Fund by the produce of a free benefit at all his theatres: affording an example that has been generally followed. The candid and liberal communications of this gentleman have enabled us to lay before our readers, the following whimsical circumstances of his infant days. He was born at *Alford*, in the county of *Lincoln*, and at six or eight weeks old, being remarkably small, was put into a hand-basket, and carried by his mother behind her husband on a double horse, from *Alford* to *Boston* (28 miles) where he made his public entry. At six years old, he performed a fairy in a pantomime, at *Lynn;* in which he ascended in a chariot to the top of the house, where he was obliged to remain till the piece was finished. Feeling himself easy and comfortable, he fell asleep, though in a critical situation, for, had he been by any accident overbalanced, he must inevitably have been dashed to pieces, as the height was very great. Here poor SHAFTOE was *forgotten*, and the *house was closed*. Being missed at supper, it was conjectured he had gone to bed; but, on enquiry, they recollected with consternation, the situation he was left in, and its danger. In this distress, his father instantly repaired to the stage-keeper's lodgings, and called him out of bed. In fear, and almost in despair, lest his son should have fallen out, with trembling steps he approached the spot; seizing the crank, he cautiously let down the vehicle, and found him still in the arms of sleep. The safety of the object ascertained, his fears gave way to an irritability of disposition, and he directly knocked him out of the chariot, which completely awaked him, and brought him to his senses. Theatricals here, were, formerly carried on in a rude building, consisting of pit and gallery, in *Westgate*. About thirty years ago, a more convenient one was erected in the *Market-Place;* but still no boxes, till, ten years back, this necessary part of uniformity was added. In 1800, when the lease expired, a new and handsome theatre was built, with two tiers of circular boxes, by JOSEPH LAWRENCE, Esq. The season is annual for five weeks, commencing n December. The house holds fifty pounds, at the prices of 3s. 2s. and 1s.

THEATRE,

LEWES.

London. Publish'd 1 June 1804 by T. Woodfall, Villiers St. Strand.

THEATRE, LEWES.

THIS Theatre is introduced more from its picturesque appearance, than from any intrinsic claim to notice. The town has been occasionally used by most of the Kentish managers ; but, from a religious tendency in its inhabitants, it is a bad resort for players. WILLIAMS, PETERS, SMITH, and Mrs. BAKER, with many others, performed here, sometimes in the town-hall, and sometimes in a barn. The veteran JEFFERSON was two seasons in WILLIAMS'S company, by the name of BURTON. He married his former wife, under a penalty of five hundred pounds, if she ever appeared upon the stage. WILLIAMS was commanded by some of the principal people of the town to get up the Funeral: Mrs. J. to personate Lady Charlotte. The bond was ineffectually urged ; for, on the knowledge of such a barrier, they actually suceeeded in prevailing on her father, Mr. MAY, of the Navy, to give it up. The ladies provided the females of the company with dresses for the piece, and it was played three nights, each person's share amounting to six guineas. DAVIES, in his Life of GARRICK, says—" Mrs. JEFFERSON was a very elegant woman, the most complete figure in beauty of countenance and symetry of form, I ever beheld; this good woman, for she was virtuous as she was fair, died suddenly at *Plymouth*, in the year 1766, as she was looking at a dance, that was practising for the night's representation ; in the midst of a hearty laugh she was seized with a sudden pain, and expired in the arms of Mr. MOODY." The first regular theatre was built by Mr. Fox, who played on the off nights of the *Brighton* season; but his involvements soon compelled him to grant a mortgage for about nine hundred pounds. After Mr. COBB had paid PAINE, as settled by the arbitration (*vide Brighton*) they still refused him the expected licence, unless he paid the mortgage, and by that means purchaseed the concern. In this dilemma, he gave a note at ten or twelve days date, but afterwards refused to honor it, as he thought it an extortion: an action was the consequence, and he was cast. He then renewed JONAS and PENLEY's lease

for

for twenty-one years, at the annual rent of fifty pounds, including the adjoining buildings, which let for, one eight and the other ten pounds per year. The present leaseholders are in possession of some small towns in the neighbourhood, of which *Eastbourne* is the chief. They annually " *show 'em in*" at *Peckham Fair*, and renew the days of THESPIS. *Bartholomew* has encountered much loss by their desertion, for these few years past. The theatre is situate at the bottom of *Star Lane*, in a place oftentimes called *Botany Bay*. Expences ten pounds, and holds seventy, at 3s. 2s. and 1s. An annual season.

DESCRIPTION OF THE PLATE.

THE large door under the portico is the only entrance to the auditory part—the stage entrance is down the lane by the hand-rail. The adjoining tenements are let to poor families—the situation is rather dirty.

THEATRE

EXETER.

London, Publish'd 1 May. 1804, by T. Woodfall, Villiers St. Strand.

THEATRE, EXETER.

THE Old House was built in 1749, and stood in *Theatre-Lane*, it was under the Management of Mr. KENNEDY, from *Bath*, who also had *Portsmouth* and *Plymouth* Theatres. About 1758, he sold it to Mr. PITT, who was nicknamed Harlequin, at whose death, the widow continued it till 1764, when Mr. JEFFERSON joined her in the Management. In 1765, JEFFERSON and JOSIAH FOOTE, a butcher, of *Exeter*, purchased the Widow's property, and renewed the lease. Mr. J. returning to *Drury-Lane* in 1767, sold also his interest to Mr. FOOTE, who thereby became the sole Proprietor; but he shortly afterwards resold a part to Mr. WOLFE. In 1787, Mr. HUGHES, the present Proprietor, with the assistance of Mr. TRUMAN, a Printer there, purchased the whole, and built the Theatre near the *Circus*. Mr. H. was bred to the *Devil and Bush*, or button painting line, at *Birmingham*, but having " *a soul above buttons, and panting for a liberal profession*," he frequented a house in that town, (JACK COTTERELL's, the Box Iron, in *Dudley-street*), where the back parlour was fitted up for the convenience of a Spouting Club.

———————————————a glorious treat,
Where 'Prentice Kings alarm the gaping street.

Here, he and Mr. SIDDONS were one evening roused to a noble pitch of emulation, by hearing that Mr. JONES, the acting manager for WARD, (grand-father to the present Mrs. SIDDONS was to be there.) They struck a bargain, and made their first appearance on the stage at *Coventry*, where they played in a Riding house, and dressed in Bridewell. HUGHES was engaged as painter and performer; and having a good study, was reckoned an useful hand. His good fortune having conducted him to *Plymouth Dock*, he married the daughter of WILLIAMS, the manager there, and is now become proprietor of that, and several other theatres. Here, as in most other Cities, the theatre is not attended in proportion to the population: the company, generally speaking, is respectable; but *Devonshire* has never yet been famous for producing theatrical geniuses. The building stands on a very eligible spot, is exceedingly pretty, and fitted up on the plan of the old SADLER's Wells, probably designed by the same artist; the proprietor being connected with that concern. The dressing-rooms are situated at the back, underneath the stage; the house will hold nearly 100*l.* at 3s. 2s. and 1s. the season towards the spring and the assize week. The Monthly Mirror says, " it is here as it is every where, might overcomes right; the manager takes all the best business to himself; the treasurer, who is likewise a performer, has the second choice; and the company scramble for what is left." The tremulous voice and manner adopted by Mr. KING in the character of *Lord Ogleby,* was an imitation of Mr. ANDREW BRICE, a printer, of this city, who had accumulated an independent fortune, but who was, in a variety of instances, a perfect model for the representative of the antiquated debauchee. GAY, the English fabulist, was born here.

DESCRIPTION OF THE PLATE.

The first door under the Portico, conducts you to the Boxes, the further one to the Pit; an ugly entrance, having a short turn at the bottom of twelve or fourteen steps; where, by proceeding forward, you gain the Stage. The Gallery entrance is on the ascent. The large semicircular Window was made after the building was finished; the Stage being found too dark for the rehearsals; the Town Arms prevented its being in the centre.

THEATRE,

London, Publish'd Oct.r 1, 1804, by T. Woodfall, Villiers St. Strand.

THEATRE ROYAL, NEWCASTLE.

MESSRS. LEE, HAMILTON, and others, from the *Edinburgh* Company, performed in a *booth* erected in the *Castle-Yard*, to which there was no pit, (the prices were, two shillings and one shilling;) at various periods from 1735 to 1750, The twenty following years were occupied by Mr. BAKER, of *York*, who sported a *booth* also, in the *Turk's Head-yard, Bigg Market*. After some time, a Theatre was built for him, which has since been converted to a Concert-room: his season was from the time of the races to the end of August: Mr. TATE WILKINSON was concerned with him the few last years of his term. In 1767; 1768, and 1769, they let the house to Messrs. AUSTIN and HEATTON, for the winter season; and the lease expiring the ensuing August, the proprietors refused them a renewal, because they declined establishing a winter company, in conformity to the custom of the three foregoing years: WILKINSON has frequently expressed regret at not complying. AUSTIN and HEATTON continued to perform; but the management undergoing frequent changes, it is evident that no new lease was granted. There were two galleries in this theatre, one of which, like the establishment of ancient *Drury*, was gratuitously meant for servants. This opening for imposition and disturbance, is now generally and commendably discontinued. The following advertisement appeared on the sixth of February at the bottom of the bills. " As many people come under the pretence of being servants, to be admitted into the upper gallery, no person will be admitted but those who are *livery servants*, and keep places in the boxes for the night." In 1772 Mr. WHITELY's name appears as manager, though it was probably only for the race week, as the other firm continued. At this period it was unlawful to take money for theatrical representations, therefore they announced a *Concert*, between the first and second parts of which, to be given *(gratis)* the Performance. We have an instance of this before us in the bill of Mr. DUNCAN (father of the excellent actress of that name, recently engaged at *Drury-Lane)*, who had an annual overflowing benefit, supported by the United Lodges of Free and accepted Masons. From 1775 to 1780, a Mr.

H 2   CUTHELL

CUTHELL had a company of much and deserved repute, in the Hall of Judicature, in the *Castle-Yard*, which held near 70*l.* We apprehend that this company performed at certain seasons, when the regular set were absent. In 1780, Mr. WHITLOCK succeeded HEATTON; in 1781, WILKINSON re-obtained the theatre for the assize week only; during the race weeks the prices have been raised to 3s. the boxes; 2s. 6d. the pit, &c. An estimate may partly be formed of the labourious life of an itinerant player, when we state that AUSTIN and WHITLOCK's circuit, consisting of *Newcastle, Lancaster, Chester, Whitehaven,* and *Preston,* occasioned the performers a necessity of travelling eleven hundred miles each year, in addition to the constant wearinesss and fatigue of studying and acting. The present theatre, which has the honour of being Royal, and which was opened with " The Way to Keep him" in 1789, was built in *Mosely-street,* by the subscription of a hundred persons, for about 6800*l.* Mr. AUSTIN retired to the neighbourhood of *Chester,* where he was very lately living; and previous to the new house's opening, MUNDEN, who had been in the company ten years, obtained his share (WHITLOCK and MUNDEN) however, in fifteen months he became tired of the management, and disposed of the property to his partner. Mr. STEPHEN KEMBLE, in 1791, bought WHITLOCK's interest in it for a thousand pound, and issued subscription tickets for 2s. 6d. the boxes, and 1s. 6d. the pit. It is let by the year, or rather season, for other exhibitions are occasionally made there, and will hold 140*l.* The stage is something larger than the *Hay-market*; the pit but small (which we think on most occasions rather improvident; for the pit is certainly the manager's best dependence for the expences of the house, though perhaps not so much so in the country as in town). The green-room and dressing-rooms are good; the gallery will hold 40*l.*; to which alone, no half price is taken: an invidious distinction in favour of those who best can afford to pay, and whose time is more at their own disposal. The season formerly commenced at Christmas, continuing to Easter; but when KEMBLE took the *Edinburgh* house, he changed it to the space from Michaelmas to January; and afterwards restored it as before, to the no small offence of many, as may be seen in his Address to the Proprietors, published in the Papers, in consequence of an advertisement in the *Newcastle Chronicle* and *Courant,* to let the Theatre to the highest bidder. In this address he states a number of reasons why he should have the preference, though he confesses there are persons coming forward, who were ready and willing to out-bid him. He was thrown out at one of their meetings, but, afterwards regained the theatre, by agreeing

to

to *come down* an extra hundred pounds a year, and not to perform at *Shields* during their season : his practice was to play at *Shields* and *Newcastle* alternately, every night ; harrassing his performers, and retarding their exertions. When he performs Job Thornberry in The Englishman's Fire Side, being unable to stoop for the waistcoat in consequence of his immensity of his size, he comes on with it, and is thereby compelled to omit one of the finest parts of the character.—Would it not be better to omit the whole ? The prices of admission are 3s. 2s. and 1s.—STEPHEN KEMBLE's circuit consists of *Newcastle*, purchased of WHITLOCK ;—*Scarborough, Durham, Sunderland, South and North Shields, and Stockton,* purchased in 1799, of CAWDELL ;—also *Darlington*—and *Coventry* is about to be added.

DESCRIPTION OF THE PLATE.

The folding Doors under the Portico is the way to the Boxes ; the entrance to the Pit, is by a door seen in the dark side of the building ; that to the Gallery, immediately opposite. The Stage Door is up the paved court on the right of the building, at the corner of which is seen the Bank of Messrs. SURTEES, BURDEN, and Co. ; the building on the left is the Post Office. In the left wing of the Theatre may be seen, evident marks of a bad foundation, which is said to have been made with ballast.

THEATRE, EDMONTON.

WE mention this Theatre, which is a barn but recently erected, merely by the way, that our friends may not have reason to accuse us of omission, even in things so totally insignificant as our present subject of meditation. It is by this insignificance that OSBORNE, the manager, stands indebted to the magistrates and managers of the *London* theatres, (within whose jurisdiction the whole of his circuit lies) for not being stopped in his career; and it would be difficult (notwithstanding our professions) to assign him a place in the " Tourist," but that he affords us an opportunity of exposing the miserable custom of *puffing*, so completely disgraceful to most of our Provincial Theatres. The company, which is small, are constantly employed either at *Woolwich,* (where is a *Theatre!*) *Enfield, Epping, Barnet,* or any village in the vicinity of *London*, where he can meet with the least encouragement. The salaries are low; twelve shillings being thought a good one. The following extract from one of his bills, will show that puffing is the substitute for merit;

" By *His Majesty's Servants,*
Theatre *Royal, Woolwich.*
DOUGLAS; or, *The Noble Shepherd,*

This night, a Douglas your protection claims,
A wife, a mother—pity's softest names!
The story of her woes, indulgent hear,
And grant your suppliant all he asks—a tear."

(He must be a liberal player who can think himself sufficiently *paid* by the *tears* of his audience.)

" REVIEW.

And Caleb Quotem (alias parish clerk, sexton, apothecary, school-master, auctioneer, engraver, plumber, glazier, painter, music-master, stone-mason, poet, and grave digger), Mr. OSBORNE." This system of puffing is arrived at an enormous height; it " shews a pitiful ambitiom in the fool that uses it," and, " though it may make the unskilful laugh; cannot but make the judicious grieve." We are sorry to say, that even *Drury-Lane* has lately betrayed a

symptom

EDMONTON.

London, Publish'd 1, Jan: 1805, by T Wewtfall, Villers S.t Strand.

symptom of infection. Has a young actor of great merit, who recently appeared, *no name*, that they give him that of *Roscius?* At *Covent Garden* they disdain the artifice. WATSON (or CARLTON) who has been termed the prince of puffers; tells us that " eighteen thousand pounds, has this play (*The Castle Spectre*) already drawn to *Drury-Lane*, and that it still continues to fill the immense space of that magnificent building." But he has been outdone by a Western Manager, as the following instances will clearly prove. " To the fashinable world. Miss GOUGH's transcendant abilities are extremely well known.; she is universally considered a second Mrs. SIDDONS, and whenever that lady retires from the stage, Miss G. will certainly succeed her at *Drury-Lane*; but *two stars cannot move in one sphere.*" Again. " From the establishment of the Drama, the wisest legislators have uniformly considered the stage, as a school of morality and decorum, and the lash of its satire as a potent ally to the magistrate in correcting vice and folly. The Irish Parliament, surrounded by calamity, occasioned by rebellion, have turned its attention to this object; and Mr. JONES, the Manager of the Theatre in *Dublin*, has actually been voted the sum of 5000*l.* to support the credit of what is called by the Lord Chancellor, a rational and proper national entertainment." It would really be a *public loss* to omit the following. In *large characters* at the top of a bill, are these words; " By Command of His Majesty and the Royal Family;" and afterwards, in *small ones*; " This Play *will be* done as soon as they *arrive at Weymouth*. (The Theatre has since been stiled Royal); we shall produce one more example from the same Theatre, and dismiss the fulsome subject. " *Richard* has always been considered one of the most difficult of SHAKESPEAR's characters. The performer who undertakes the task must bring to it a mature judgment and extensive powers; the most skillfull discrimination, and an exhaustless spirit; blunt, yet hypocritical; barbarous and unrelenting, but occasionally checked by the still voice of conscience, an ardent lover, but a tyrannical husband; frightened by a dream, and yet disdaining to be subdued by it; suspicious, yet daring politic in counsel, and courageous in the field of battle. Arduous as a character thus versatile must be, it is yet one of the most favourable parts which an able actor can possibly select for the display of his abilities.

Such a man is *****.

Who not only *thinks* originally, but *looks, speaks,* and *walks* unlike any other actor on the stage,—in short,

" *We shall not look upon his like again.*"—" *He is himself alone.*"

N. B. This is but one fourth of the original—

O Tempora O Mores! THEATRE.

THEATRE, MAIDSTONE.

IN 1757 WIGNALL, an under actor at *Covent-Garden*, collected a sharing company for the summer season ; among whom were the late TATE WILKIN-SON, JEFFERSON, Miss HALLAM (now Mrs. MATTOCKS), Miss MORRISON, (now Mrs. HULL) Mr. HULL, Mr. JONES, &c. &c. There had been no theatricals before for many years. In the *Star Yard*, he erected a wooden booth, and opened to five pounds. Names such as those above, inspire a regret at such success, or rather want of it, for frequently the receipts were found unequal to defray the charge, and the scanty audience was of course dismissed. In some weeks the shares were not *six shillings* each ; and WIL-KINSON netted at his benefit, by The Distrest Mother, *two pieces of candle* and *eighteen-pence.* In conseqnence of a supposed plan laid by the Manager, and Mr. and Mrs. BARRINGTON, to secure to themselves a decent benefit, by certain measures that would prove injurious to the rest, the aggrieved parties drew up the following resolution, which was regularly signed and notified : " That as the playhouse, in the *Star Yard, Maidstone*, was so ill attended, and as there were so many sufferers, they could not, and would not proceed, or act any more in that booth, for the emolument of two or three persons ; as to continue a fortnight longer, would plunge them all into the utmost penury and want." This serious remonstrance had the desired effect ; an amicable adjustment immediately took place ; the rebellious subjects returned to their allegiance, and the manager once more meditated on the profits of the *Assize Week*, which, were before in imminent danger. By virtue of this treaty the company were allowed a share of the benefits in question, each of which pro-duced the *enormous sum* of *nineteen or twenty pounds*, thereby finishing much more decently than they expected. Nevertheless, JONES and another were obliged to paint their way out of the town, being reduced by the miserable profits of the season, to furnish *Signs* to those who would employ them. *Canterbury* SMITH amused the people in 1762. This man, from an idea that his son resembled the greatest actor in the country ; and looking forward to

his

MAIDSTONE.

London, Publish'd Dec.r 1.1804 by I. Wendall, Villiers St. Strand.

THEATRE

becoming another Roscius, had him christened GARRICK: Mr. BROWN succeeded him. Mrs. BAKER, the present Proprietor, has had possession about thirty years. At first, she rented by the season, a large warehouse at the corner of *High-street*, near the water side, belonging to Mr. MERCER, and fitted it up on the principle of the now existing theatre. It frequently happened (being so near the river) that the tide prevented her performing, or opening the doors for weeks, The new theatre in *High-street*, opposite the *Conduit*, was opened on Thursday, the 12th of April 1798, with " Every One has his Fault," " Gaffer's Mistake," (an Interlude by DIBDIN), and " The Prize." It is freehold property; cost 1300*l.* the building, and 600*l.* the ground ;—holds 60*l.* at 3s. 2s. and 1s.; the boxes, in the second Act, 2s. by a new Arithmetic, termed *half-price*. The Season returns but once in two or three years ; by which means, the inhabitants are never cloyed. Mr. T. DIBDIN brought out at his benefit, his popular piece of " The Jew and the Doctor," under the name of " The Jew Guardian," on the 12th of July 1798. Abednego, DOWTON ; Old Bromley, T. BIBDIN, &c. &c. ; the first and last time of its representation, till performed in London. Mr. RICHARDSON, a friend of Mr. HARRIS, being present, was so much pleased with both the Farce and Author, that he recommended them to him in the warmest manner. The Company went from hence to *Tunbridge Wells*, where Mr. DIBDIN received a letter, intimating that Mr. HARRIS would be glad to see him. The interview was attended with mutual satisfaction, and his " Mouth of the Nile" soon afterwards appeared. The late Duke of LEEDS, was so much gratified with the works of this writer, " The Tight little Island," " The Land in the Ocean," &c. that he honoured him with his patronage as long as he lived, and considerably assisted him in his views with HARRIS. The productions of this Author are too well known, and too deservedly admired, to receive additional celebrity from any observations that we can make respecting them ; nevertheless, it is but just to declare, that his touches of wit and humour, are those of a Master ; and well relieved by a judicious adaption of sentiment : his works prove him a scholar, and his manners, a Gentleman.

DESCRIPTION OF THE PLATE.

The center of the folding door used for the shop of a Fruiterer, is the only external admission ;—the plan of all Mrs. BAKER's Theatres. The two side doors are opened at the close of performances, for the more expeditiously clearing the House.

I.   THEATRE,

THEATRE ROYAL, LIVERPOOL.

MR. HEARNE, an old Actor, had a small sharing Company in *Lancashire*, and occasionally came to *Liverpool*. There was afterwards a Theatre which was rented by GIBSON, of *Covent Garden*, situated in *Drury Lane*, holding about 70*l*. A History of *Chester*, published in 1791, says, the late Theatre at *Liverpool* is now occasionally used as a Conventicle by some Dissenters.— On the 10th of January 1770, a petition of WILLIAM GIBSON, for a Playhouse, (supported by a petition of the Mayor, Aldermen, and Common Council, praying the bill might pass) went through the Commons; but, upon the question for Committing it in the Lords, it was rejected. This petition was in January 1771, more successfully followed by another, for the bill passed both Houses, and terminated in a patent. A new Theatre was built in *Williamson-Square*, very near the former, at the expence of the Corporation, on behalf of GIBSON, who died before it was completed. His loss was much lamented as being the first who raised the *Liverpool* Theatricals to consequence; and as being what is infinitely better, an example of benevolence, but rarely to be met with. He left a donation of considerable amount to the indigent of the town, and was buried about three miles from *Liverpool*, where YOUNGER, and several other persons of the Drama, are intered. GARRICK has contributed to perpetuate his memory, by the lines inscribed on his tomb. BAKER states that he left part of his property to the *Covent Garden* Fund; but, we believe the truth to be, that he bequeathed the greatest portion of his fortune to Mrs. BENNETT, with whom he had lived for many years, and the *reversion* of it to the fund, at her disease. The new Theatre opened on Friday, June the 5th, 1772, with a Prologue, written by the elder COLMAN, which contains the following lines, applicable to the intended Manager.

" Peace to his shade, who first pursued the plan;
You loved the actor, and you loved the man.
True to himself—to all mankind a friend,
By honest means he's gained an honest end.
You, like kind patrons, who his wishes knew,
Prompt to applaud, and to reward them too,
Crowned his last moments with his wish obtained;
A Royal Charter, by your bounty gained."

YOUNGER

LIVERPOOL.

London, Publish'd Dec.r 1, 1804, by T. Woodfall, Villiers S.t Strand.

YOUNGER and MATTOCKS had the Theatre in 1775, with KNIVETON, who had some share in it. YOUNGER was fond of acting, notwithstanding his impediment of an obstinate lisp. The public, however, were much indebted to him for introducing that valuable acquisition to to the stage, the elegant Miss FARREN. He met with her, when barely entering her teens, in a barn, where she was delivering GEORGE ALEXANDER STEVENS's Lecture upon Heads, to supply the necessities of herself, her mother, and her sister. YOUNGER was struck with the *toute ensemble*, and prevailed on Mrs. FARREN to article her daughter to himself (it being a condition to maintain the family till the articles expired), and brought her out at *Covent Garden*, at which Theatre he was Prompter. Let no fastidious critic sneer, and condemn us as the exposers of events that ought to be forgotten;—we rather conceive that we have fulfilled our duty in announcing to the world that *virtue is rewarded*. *Liverpool*, from its trade, situation, and other advantages, may generally be considered a successful resort: the receipts of the season of 1782, amounted to 3000*l*. and in 1784, to 3746*l*. Mr. YOUNGER died a few weeks after his benefit, and Mr. MATTOCKS became sole Manager. A mischievous spirit one night threw a knife from the gallery at HOLLINGSWORTH, who was peeping through the curtain, which narrowly missed his eye. When LEE, the son of a *Liverpool* blacksmith, an effeminate character, was to have played the first *speaking* part, (Mat o'the Mint), BARRYMORE, who was the Macheath of the evening, being imperfect, to his unspeakable mortification, cut him entirely out; and when the Manager enquired how it happened that the scene was omitted, he coolly replied that LEE had not studied it, and therefore he passed it by. Mr. LEE, is now strutting and fretting at *Covent Garden*, where tricks have been frequently practised upon him with the greatest effect. The occasion that brought Mr. WEBB of *Drury-Lane*, to exhibit his *graces* before a *London* audience, was as follows:—When Major HALLIDAY performed the part of the Bastard, to KEMBLE's King John, WEBB was to play the Citizen who speaks from the walls; and he recited at morning rehearsal, the very long speech originally written by SHAKESPEARE, but omitted in representation. Mr. KEMBLE advised him to conform to the practice in *London*; and stated the aukward situation of the principal characters in case of refusal. WEBB nodded assent: but, in the evening delivered the whole faithful to his Author in every letter, and was rewarded with abundant applause. KEMBLE who had measured his strides, and his stops, and his starts, with the nicest precision, to eke out the quantity given in *London*, was much disconcerted through the rest of

the

the scene; but WEBB was soon afterwards engaged for the seat of the Muses. In 1786, Captain ASH made his appearance in Captain Macheath. In the first Act, he wore a morning dress; a full dress in the second; and a suit of black in the last; he had a clean shirt for every Act; an instance of cleanliness only to be excelled by that of a brother Captain who washed his money. This process, for which the Green Room was allotted him, detained the audience between the acts, a good half hour. Mr. AIKIN commenced Manager in 1787. KEMBLE had it for the season of 1789 only. A portico was about that time added, as a necessary shelter for the company in rainy weather. The house used to be open during the time that the *London* Theatres were closed, and the principal performers of the latter, were, in consequence selected. Formerly, no actor, of whatever rank, could be permitted to appear here, without a regular engagement for the season; the townsmen having made a successful resistance to the introduction of Provincial Performers in the summer, of whom Mrs. SIDDONS and JOHN KEMBLE formed a part;—the latter was hissed off the stage, after addressing the audience in this manner, " Shall I tell you what you are like? You are like Captain Driver, in *Oroonoko*; and Mrs. S. who had frequently played here in the winter and was favourably received in both the walks of Tragedy and Comedy, was (as the event proves, *fortunate for herself*) compelled to leave the town; but such is the versitility of public favour and of public sentiments, that, on her re-appearance, after having received the stamp of approbation from a *London* audience, those who had been most instrumental in her dismission, were now so eager to witness her performance, that many persons sustained considerable injury. It is nothing unusual to wish to be exempted from the trouble of thinking for ourselves. An annual benefit is given to the public charities; also to an old Manager of the name of HURST. In the year 1798, died that most accomplished actor Mr. JOHN PALMER, while *performing* the character of the Stranger; of whom it may perhaps be truly said, " He was a MAN—that, take him for *all in all*, we ne'er shall look upon his like again,"

    Like a staunch ve'tran, in himself a host,

    Game to the last, he perished at his *post.*

He was buried close by GIBSON. WILD, the Prompter, died on the 10th of August, 1801. He was desirous of being intered at Liverpool, and pointed out the spot, a long time previous to his disease. Mr. AIKIN's lease having expired and he being universally disliked; and the scenery, wardrobe, and orchestra very bad; Messrs. LEWIS and KNIGHT, of *Covent Garden*, took the

                   Theatre

Theatre in 1803, for fourteen years, under a number of restrictions, at the yearly rent of 1500*l.* ; AIKIN had it for 360*l.* only ; and the *Proprietor of this Work*, actually offered, before the expiration of AIKIN's lease 700*l.* per annum ; when he received for answer, that if he thought proper to *double* his proposal, he would *then* be treated with. When this Theatre was built, the back part extended to a rope walk, and might have been continued to any depth, there being nothing to impede it. A narrow street has been since built, in such a manner that the back of the Theatre forms a part of one of its sides. There is now, therefore, no possibility of gaining room that way, though it is much required. Its late protrusion into the square, very much hurts the appearance of the latter ; which, had it not been the property of the Corporation, would never have been suffered. They usually play four nights per week ; six in the race week. Their first season lasted upwards of ten months, including summer and winter. Last year it was found expedient to reduce the salaries—the highest is now *two pounds* ; for this purpose, they had two sets of printed articles ; one for the summer, and the other for the winter engagements. The charges for the summer benefits, are *sixty* guineas ; for the winter *fifty-five.* The success that young BETTY experienced at this place, exceeded credibility. He drew fourteen or fifteen houses of nearly 300*l.* each night ; the last of which was more crowded than the first. He cleared 1520*l.* The following night, with the attraction of " Guilty or not Guilty," a new Piece, they performed to *twenty pounds* ; and so bad were the houses afterwards, that they prematurely closed the season, which was to have gone on till May. They usually begin in June. The people of *Liverpool*, though opulent, having acquired vast sums by trade, are not the most enlightened. They are, as is natural under such circumstances, prejudiced and tenacious, (of which we have already given an example) though they are extremely generous wherever they approve. When GARRICK performed in BEN JOHNSON's Comedy of " Every Man in his Humour," the Piece was highly patronized ; notwithstanding this, a few years after, when that play was revived, the good people insisted it had never been done, as unworthy of representation. Some years ago, the Tragedy of Oroonoko was prohibited, as reflecting too much on their conduct, in the practice of the Slave Trade.— Much might have been added to our account of this Theatre ; but, an unaccommodating spirit in those persons to whom we applied for information ; and who were most capable of communicating it, compels us, unwillingly, to omit much matter, that would, doubtless, be acceptable to the readers of a theatrical production.

THEATRE.

THEATRE, WINDSOR.

IS a Theatre Royal; which can scarcely be said to enjoy a regular season, as it greatly depends upon the time of His Majesty's residence, who is almost its only support: the few stationary performances take place in June. Lower Boxes 4s. Upper ditto 3s. 6d. Slips 3s. Pit 2s. and Gallery 1s.—second prices 2s. 6d. 1s. 6d. 1s. and 6d. and holds about 70*l*. The Green Room is a continuation of the Stage, with rooms beneath. On the left, is a private house, which serves His Majesty for an avenue, whenever he honours the Theatre with his presence. It is recorded in the Playhouse companion for 1764, that Mrs. CENTLIVRE, the Dramatist, whose name at that time was CARROL, performed in this town, the part of Alexander the Great, in 1706. Mr. JOSEPH CENTLIVRE, one of QUEEN ANNE's cooks, fell in love with, and married her. In 1748, YATES opened a theatrical booth. From 1778 to 1793, the lovers of the Drama experienced much inconvenience on account of the Theatre being situated near a mile from the town, in a dirty farm yard, at the bottom of *Pescod-street*. This *house*, which was literally a *barn*, held about 25*l*. no boxes in front. WALDRON, commander, BENSON, the hero. It is difficult to conceive how so remote a situation could struggle through a period of fifteen years, in so bad a theatrical neighbourhood. It is worthy of remark, that the Theatre never was graced with the Royal Presence till after it was removed; which then it patronized; a powerful instance of the folly of that man who builds a playhouse at a distance from those persons who only can support it. One morning, in consequence of a performer having been engaged from *London*, for half a dozen nights, who played some of Mrs. BENSON's characters; the indignant hero thought proper to be absent; and WALDRON was compelled to post to Richmond, (sixteen or seventeen miles, in a cross country road) in order to procure a substitute; Seven o'clock arrived; but not the Manager. The house being full, they protracted the time by beginning with the Farce—at length the Farce was finished, and no arrival—a comic song, still no arrival— then an Epilogue, when he appeared; and bringing with him LESTRANGE, the Play proceeded. Here WALDRON is said to have performed the Suspicious Hus-

band,

WINDSOR.

London, Publish'd 1.Feb.ʸ 1803 by T.Wensfield Villiers S.ᵗ Strand.

THEATRE ROYAL

band, and She Stoops to Conquer, without a Mr. Strickland in the one ; and Miss Hardcastle in the other. Having lent to BENSON some scenery for a country scheme, the hero, in return, got Windsor from him ; though WALDRON's own account is, that he sold his interest to Mr. C. STEVENS, formerly of *Covent Garden.* Mr. W. was accustomed to take volunteer performers from the Richmond Company, on the off nights to play at Windsor about five or six weeks, annually, in coaches. In one of these journeys, a shower coming on, WALDRON, who was on the outside, with several of the band, attempted to force a bass viol for shelter and protection, into the interior, which being already incommoded with six grown persons beside some children, occasioned a formidable opposition. A regular, well-conducted, and successful attack was immediately made on the intruding instrument, and the lamenting sons of Orpheus, beheld its speedy and utter demolition. When Mrs. WILSON went from *Richmond*, accompanied by WILLIAMS, to play the " Country Girl." Mrs. ***L***, who had received no previous notice, and who always represented that character, was so enraged, that forgetting the *delicate softness* of her sex, she seized a duck, then roasting for her dinner, and that of her *chere ami*, and threw it at him, who, not to be behind hand, snatched a horse whip from Mr. WILLIAMS, and flourished it most dexterously round her ribs. On the first of August, 1793, the old Theatre, under the mangement of BENSON, gave place to the present, situate in *High-street*, which opened under the direction of Mr. THORNTON, with " Every one has his Fault," succeeded by Rosina. Mr. T. is of opinion that six bad nights per week, are better than three middling ones, and consequently *works* his actors. The following may be added to the eccentricities of this superlatively singular being. After playing Bulcazin Muley, in the Mountaineers, before his Royal Patrons, he was commanded to attend the Castle for further orders. He instantly undressed, put on a great coat, and went to the appointment. Being ushered into the room in which he usually received instructions, he knelt to address an illustrious Personage, who instantly burst into a fit of laughter, and suddenly retired : furnishing the wonderstruck dependant with a fine dramatic incident. Much disconcerted, he returned, ruminating on the cause of this so strange occurrence ; when, by accident, a looking glass developed the foregoing mystery— his countenance was decorated with an enormous pair of whiskers, and besmeared with ochre, just as he had personated the Moorish Chief. THORNTON has repeatedly endeavoured to dispose of this concern ; and has lately *taken in* a Mr. DAVENPORT as partner.

THEATRE,

THEATRE, CHICHESTER.

A Company under the Management of Mr. DYMER, formerly played at a room in an Inn, in this *City*. Mrs. CHARKE says in her life, published in 1755, that she " was once requested by a person in the pit, while playing the part of *Pyrrhus*, to give them some speeches out of *Scrub*, which she had performed the night before, with great success." A curious specimen of *refined judgement*, and *theatrical taste*, in the amateurs of former days. It was left to GARRICK not only to reform and grace the Stage, but also to direct and ripen the ideas of an audience. Mr. DYMER was succeeded in 1764, by Mr. SAMUEL JOHN-STONE, who converted a Malthouse into a tolerable Theatre, holding about 40*l*. COLLINS and DAVIS were the next Campaigners. In 1792, a very pretty Theatre holding 50*l*. was erected by tontine, on the scite of the old one. His Grace the Duke of RICHMOND, whose seat (at *Goodwood*) is near *Chichester*, superintended the building, and generously furnished it, when completed, with some beautiful scenery, painted by first rate artists, for his private Theatre in *Privy Garden*. It has an annual, productive season, seldom playing above three nights a week. The salaries run from eighteen shillings to a guinea and a half; and the performers take their benefits by two and two: charges 17*l*. Admissions 3s. 2s. and 1s.

THEATRE,

CHICHESTER.

London. Publish'd 1 Jany 1805. by T.Woodfall, Villiers St Strand.

SHAKSPEARE
Hotel & Tavern

London, Published 1 Feb.r 1805, by T. Woodfall, Villiers S.t Strand.

BIRMINGHAM.

THEATRE, BIRMINGHAM.

THEATRICAL Exhibitions in *Birmingham* are rather of modern date, none being on record till after the commencement of the eighteenth century, and those (to use the corrupted state of the word) of a truly *Brummagem* kind. Some strollers erected a temporary shed of boards and canvass in the fields (that part of them which now forms *Temple-street*). About 1730, the amusements of the Stage attained a superior degree of credit; for the itinerant heroes opened a barn, or stable, in the Castle-yard, where they performed in painted rags and tinselled ornaments, to an audience replete with boisterous mirth, who went to banish care at *three-pence* a head. The first regular Theatre was erected ten years afterwards, in *Moor-street*, which gave another spring to the proceedings: in the day-time, a *drum* paraded the town for Volunteers for night, who beat his rounds, delivered his bills, and roared out encomiums on the entertainments, which, however, had not always the desired effect. We have been informed by an eye-witness of the fact, that the celebrated YATES has filled this office; and when we reflect that both himself and SHUTER exercised their talents in a booth in Bartholomew Fair, astonishment ceases. The house was afterwards converted into a conventicle, where WESLEY sometimes thumped the cushion; it then became a grocer's warehouse; and ultimately the workshop of Messrs. BELLAMY and Co. In 1751, a handsome Theatre was built in *King-street*, and opened in 1752, by a company announcing themselves *His Majesty's Servants from the Theatres Royal, London*. These persons expressed a wish that the townsmen would excuse the ceremony of the drum, alledging as a reason *the dignity of a London Company*. The novelty had a surprising effect; the performers pleased, and the house was continually crowded: the general conversation turned upon theatricals; and the town seemed to exhibit one vast theatre. Encouraged by this success, a rivalship was established by a *second* London company; but soon perceiving that the public were unable or unwilling to patronise two theatres, they withdrew their claim. In June 1762, Messrs. HULL and YOUNGER had a sharing

K   company.

company. In June 1774, an opposition was again attempted, and a Theatre opened in *New-street*, under the management of Mr. YATES, with "As you like it," Touchstone by himself, after a Prologue written by FOOTE. In 1776, MATTOCKS petitioned the Commons to grant a license; and the change of the *Birmingham* taste may be gathered from the inhabitants presenting a *counter-petition*. The matter being examined before a Committee, was there thrown out, and no further proceedings took place. About 1777, *King-street* Theatre underwent alterations, being materially improved and enlarged; but after a few nights performance it was shut up, together with its rival in *New-street*, by Justice PARSONS. The company at each house was truly respectable; but so many benefit tickets were imposed by their Masters upon the manufacturing poor, that at length it became a serious oppression. The *shilliug* admissions thus forced on the honest industrious workmen, were frequently sold to the bakers for a *sixpenny loaf* to feed their necessitous offspring. In one of the contests between YOUNGER and YATES, Mr. Ross was engaged for a certain number of nights in aid of the former. The business being bad, Ross, out of humour, wished to decline completing his engagement: the Manager, in hopes of better success, refused compliance; and being obliged to attend his duty in *London*, he strictly desired his deputy not to dismiss the house if it produced a single shilling. The "Fair Penitent" being announced, Ross went to examine the box-book, and found it a perfect blank. Concluding by this the perform-ance would not take place, he ordered a late dinner, determined to indulge. At the time the piece was about to commence, lo, there was no Horatio! A note was dispatched to require immediate attendance; to which he returned a verbal reply, and sent some one to spy out the state of the house, which was then so bad, that he resolved to stay where he was. A peremptory order was the consequence, that he should come and fulfil his engagement; whereupon he arose, went angrily to the theatre, put on a red coat and waistcoat and a wig, retaining his black satin breeches, white stockings, and dirty shoes, which he had worn all day. In the quarrelling scene, he gave the deputy Manager, who played Lothario, so severe a blow, that he absolutely sent him off the stage. When he afterwards required the reason of the insult, Ross, with af-fected ignorance, replied, " Insult! I don't remember—how ?"—" Why, Sir, the blow you gave me."—" Blow, Sir !" (rejoined the other, considering) " blow !—Oh, Sir, I felt the *animation of the part*, that was all—but no blow, Sir, no blow."——In 1779, we find the two houses again in contest, MAT-TOCKS at the old Theatre, against MILLER at the new. MILLER had property, and mounted his hobby behind the scenes; but he never could prevail on his

audience

audience to believe him the actor he imagined himself to be. After some time he was fully convinced of his error; for, in the representation of the part of Hamlet, he received repeated tokens of disapprobation. The enraged actor, in imitation of " Mr. Bayes," exclaimed aloud, " If you do not approve of my Hamlet, I solemly assure you that I never will favour an audience again with my performance of Frenchmen," (which was certainly beyond mediocrity).— The audience laughed and hissed, and Miller kept his word. *King-street* was finally knocked up in 1780, and, like many of its kind, became, and remains a meeting for Dissenters. An additional and superb portico was at this time erected, which might have justified the New-street Theatre in being pronounced one of the first Provincials in the kingdom. On the 18th of August 1792, this beautiful Theatre was destroyed by fire, but whether by design or accident has never been duly ascertained: it was discovered to be in flames about two in the morning, and by four it was reduced to an indistinguishable heap of ruins. There was reason to believe it proceeded from the diabolical malice of some incendiary; whereupon, the Proprietors offered a reward of an hundred pounds, which they afterwards doubled, to discover the infamous perpetrator. By this accident, a number of persons were seriously injured by loss of benefits, &c. &c.—The years 1793 and 1794 necessarily have been a blank in the theatrical records; but 1795 produced a stucture richer than the former, which, like a Phœnix, issued from it's Ashes. It was opened by Mr. Macready, from *Covent Garden*, with the aid of an excellent Company, on the 18th of June. Two Busts, in relief, of excellent workmanship, were elevated over the little windows, of Shakespear and Garrick, the father and refiner of the British Stage. The head of Garrick is placed in the *right wing*, by a blunder of the Architect. A beautiful Assembly Room has communication with the Boxes; and there are other commodious rooms in front, which are used for the Shakespear Tavern and Coffee-house, kept by a Mr. Wilday. The stage is not proportioned to the house, being but forty-eight feet long, and fifty wide, which causes large blank piers on each side to fill up, greatly to the prejudice of its harmony and beauty. The form of the Theatre is nearly that of half a circle; it has two tiers of boxes that go all round; and a gallery of the same shape, above. The scenes are richly painted by Messrs. Greenwood and Dixon, and the house is illuminated with wax candles, in twenty chandeliers, and patent lamps: handsome green-room, wardrobe, dressing-rooms, &c. The prices of admission are 4s. 2s. and 1s.; expences are fifty guineas; and the largest sum the house has been known to hold was 268l. 4s.: the 14th night of Master Betty's appearance. In January 1801,

some

some Ladies and Gentlemen performed two Plays, under the regulation of Mr. BISSETT; one for the benefit of the General Lying-in Hospital, and the other for the Soup Shop. MACREADY is a spirited Manager; and, during his season, which is from the middle of June to the end of September (for Birmingham never flourished as a winter Theatre), he engages the principal performers from both houses in *London*, and frequently at a great expence. There is a triennial Oratorio, for the benefit of the Fund of the General Hospital, performed in St. Philip's church; and Concerts, which are held at the Theatre, when the stage is boxed up to the ceiling: they are generally well attended. When trade is good, the Theatre flourishes; but for two or three seasons the receipts have been indifferent. The pedestals on the top of the Theatre were intended to support the figures of the Tragic and Comic Muse; but they are not now talked of.

Mr. KEMBLE is reckoned to be twenty minutes longer in his performance of Hamlet than most of his contemporaries; but Mr. DODD, when he played that part in this Theatre, was twenty minutes longer than Mr. KEMBLE;—so much for speaking looks, and dignity of pause! When MACREADY first took the Theatre, his accounts were regularly submitted to the inspection of the Proprietors, who received a third of the profits. He afterwards made a more advantageous arrangement, reserving the whole to himself on paying 700*l.* as an annual consideration for rent. COLLINS, the ingenious author and reciter of the Evening Brush, now lives at *Birmingham*, and conducts a newspaper. This is the first English Theatre at which young BETTY appeared. He shared with the Manager, after the expences, for six nights, playing a seventh gratis; which engagement was renewed. Concluding that any thing relating to this extraordinary youth will be acceptable to our readers, we shall finish our account of this Theatre with a statement of the receipts of the thirteen nights on which he played; by which it will be perceived how much his attraction increased; or rather that at first his attraction was nothing at all, for it were wrong to conceive that from 80*l.* to 100*l.* is uncommon for *Birmingham*;—

1. Night	*l.* 76 6 0	—Douglas	8 Night *l.*142 3 0—Romeo
2 ——	117 3 0	—Rolla	9 —— 261 5 6—Achmet
3 ——	95 8 6	—Hamlet	10 —— 244 12 6—Frederick
4 ——	80 5 6	—Richard	11 —— 170 14 0—Hamlet
5 ——	222 13 0	—Hamlet	12 —— 234 13 6—Octavian
6 ——	181 13 6	—Osman	13 —— 268 4 0—Richard
7 ——	193 9 6	—Douglas	

THEATRE,

London, Published 1 Feb. 1803, by T. Woodfall, Villiers St. Strand.

BOXES

MANCHESTER.

THEATRE ROYAL, MANCHESTER.

PLAYS have been performed in various parts of this populous and flourishing Town ; first, in a large room over the Exchange ; then, in a building, in *Water-street, Salford*, since used as a Riding School ; and for the last thirty years, occupied as a timber *depot*, by Mr. JOHN BERRY, a dealer in that commodity ; but the Theatre, which was superceded by the present, was the corner of *Brown* and *Marsden-streets*, neatly fitted up, under the management of Mr. WHITELY, who had been the approved dramatic caterer, for many years.   In 1765, the facetious EDWIN, made his first appearance on a public stage, under the jurisdiction of Mr. LEE : whom, in the following year, WHITELY succeeded.   There is no Manager, not even the eccentric THORNTON, to whom so many whimsicalities may be imputed ; but what is generally termed goodness of heart, effectually counterpoised the errors of his understanding, and however marvellous or irregular his actions may appear ; there are, nevertheless, among them, some of such dignified a nature, as would do honour, even to the throne.   He valued himself on being able to play any part of SHAKESPEARE's pieces, without a *double*.   He was an actor of indifferent merit ; zealous for the ancient school ; had an unseemly twitch in his deportment ; grave and sententious on all occasions, and a strict adherent to the measured cadence of te ti tum, and tum ti te.   When EDWIN applied to him for an engagement, he gave him an excellent lecture on the profession of an actor, which every performer would do well to consider, before he ventures on the *London* boards, (See EDWIN's Life, by PASQUIN, Vol. I. page 242.) This lecture was delivered at BOWDEN's theatrical public-house (the father of the singer), in November 1766.   We will relate an Anecdote of WHITELY, and then dismiss him for the present.   In a journey to *Stamford*, to save expences, he walked, and carried his portmanteau on his arm : within a few miles of his place of destination, he saw a hearse, and bargained with the driver to take him up.   Being weary, he got into the interior and fell fast asleep ; having previously desired *Jehu* to call him when he approached the town.   The arch

whip

whip anticipating the pleasure of a joke, drove into the Inn-yard, (the George) at *Stamford*, and collecting together as many of W*HITELY*'s friends as he could muster, told them he'd *show 'm fun*—then, opening the door, he waked the snorting Manager with news of his journey's end. J*EMMY* got out, and to his astonishment, perceived himself surrounded with a number of acquaintance, who all at once vociferated " Ah, Master W*HITELY* ! How do you do ? Welcome to *Stamford*." To which the disconcerted W*IGHT* replied, in his usual phrase—you lie you lie you thieves—" I am *not* Master W*HITELY* : *I do'nt know any such person*;" and coolly walked off with his portmanteau. After our Manager had enjoyed his dignity about six or seven years longer, he was supplanted by Y*OUNGER* and M*ATTOCKS*, who obtained a *Patent*, in consequence of a Petition sent to Parliament, by the Gentry, Merchants, and others, resident at *Manchester*. A new Theatre had previously been erected, in *Spring Gardens*, by subscription of fifty pounds a piece, for forty shares ; each of which is now, well worth 200*l.* as they yield no less than 22*l.* 10s. per Cent. on the original sum ; besides affording free admission to any part of the house. It is a plain brick edifice, scarcely worthy of a town of so much eminence, 102 feet long, by 48, which is extremely incommodious. It was opened in Whitsuntide week, 1774, with the Tragedy of Othello, by a Company from *London*. Mr. Y*OUNGER* continued Manager for several years, and was succeeded by a number of adventurers, none of whom continued above two seasons, till Messrs. B*ANKS* and W*ARD* assumed the managerial truncheon. An Amphitheatre was opened on the plan of A*STLEY*, in 1793, to amuse the public, during the theatrical recess. Early in the season of 1800, a Pamplet, entitled " A Peep into the Theatre Royal," was published, and created much dispute and criticism. Mr. C*ROSS*, a performer, whom it injured, answered it in an expostulatory Address. The same year, Mr. B*ANKS* relinquished his situation, in favour of Mr. B*ELLAMY*, the I*NCLEDON* of *Dublin*, who is by no means a favourite with the people ; with whom, and W*ARD*, the management rests at present. The season commences in December, and closes the latter end of June. Admissions, 3s. 2s, and 1s. no half price. The house has been known to hold (at the benefit of Mrs. W*ARD*) 129*l. Manchester* is certainly, one of the nurseries for *London*. In July 1786, Mr. M*ATTOCKS*, who shortly after failed, brought the Company, though out of the usual season, for the sake of the performance of Mrs. S*IDDONS*. Her six nights produced, 64*l.* 89*l.* 92*l.* 67*l.* 77*l.* and 78*l.* H*ER-BERT* and R*OBERTSON*, were in partnership a short time, with Y*OUNGER* and M*ATTOCKS*. H*ERBERT*, one night, represented Douglas in Henry the Fourth ;

and

and Nathaniel, his son, Sir Walter Blunt. In the fifth act where Blunt is slain, HERBERT, who seldom attended to either the words or business of his part, fell down, instead of Nathaniel. A voice from behind, *cursing his old soul*, and advising him of his error, caused him to spring up and renew the combat, when Sir Walter expired amidst the shouts and acclamations of the audience. In 1801, the Theatre was decorated, and newly painted. Theatrical Critiques were published throughout the last two seasons, which the performers contended were *very severe!* The present lease not having long to run, MACREADY and others, are on the sharp *look out*; but it is thought that LEWIS and KNIGHT will be the successful candidates. This Circuit (consisting of *Shrewsbury*, *Chester*, and *Litchfield*, as well as *Manchester*,) occupies nearly ten months in a year: for the remaining two, the majority of the performers engage at *Buxton*. It is, on the whole, a very respectable Company.

EXPLANATION OF THE PLATE.

The Centre Door on the dark side of the Drawing is the entrance to the Pit; to the Stage Door is by a small door in a low wall beyond the building; the Gallery and Box entrances are noted by the writing above them.

THEATRE,

THEATRE, SOUTHAMPTON.

So recently as 1756, Theatres were hardly known at *Portsmouth, Southampton, Chichester,* and *Winchester*: the first company of any note was that of Mr. FARREN, the father of Lady Derby, who performed at the *Town-Hall* with considerable success, till 1766, when a regular Theatre, holding about 40*l.*, was constructed from a silk mill, by subscription of the inhabitants, and the management given to Mr. SAMUEL JOHNSON: it opened in August, and closed at the end of October. The concern came shortly afterwards under the direction of COLLINS and DAVIES, who enlarged the building, and considerably improved it; for though it was neat, it was certainly much too small. About 1783, INCLEDON made his first appearance upon any stage; Mr. ROYLE, a member of the South Hants Band, first introduced him to theatrical life. Coming to the Three Tuns in this town, they called for some bread and cheese and beer: a gentleman present, applying himself to ROYLE, said, " Don't you belong to the band ?" To which he replied, " I do."—" So do I," uttered INCLEDON.—" You !" returned the other, " a *band-itti,* I suppose you mean."—Apollo assured them it was true, and that he had just come from on board of ship, with a party of singers and musicians. This was sufficient; a *specimen* was loudly called for in proof of his assertion, with which he readily complied. In short, he acquitted himself in such a manner, as induced the musician to recommend him to the Theatre, where, after being heard, he was engaged at 10s. 6d. per week, to sing an occasional song. His situation becoming unpleasant, and the Manager apprehending his daughter in danger, GRANT, a musician, who played at the Theatre, and also at Bath in the concerts, spoke for him to KEASBURY, who thought him unnecessary while he had WORDSWORTH.—" But, Sir," said GRANT, " WORDSWORTH is *lofty* at times, and this is the man to *take him down.*" He was engaged; and in getting up " Robin Hood," proposed to personify " Edwin." The Company sneered, and declared the piece would be damned:

however,

SOUTHAMPTON.

London, Publish'd 1 Feb 1801 by T.Woodfall, William S.t Strand.

however, in the song of "Since all my hopes, dear maid," he excited the feelings of the audience to such a degree, that they scarcely knew how to suppress their encores and their plaudits. It is needless to follow him further. WORDSWORTH is now explanator of the Ergascopia at the Lyceum, besides his place at the Opera.—COLLINS and DAVIES had also the *Salisbury* Theatre : the latter died in 1797, leaving eight children ; JAMES LEYTON, the eldest (a wild one), died at sea. COLLINS was left executor, whose second son (THOMAS, of *Drury-lane)* married HENRIETTA DAVIES, the second daughter. Some of the children have still an interest in the concern, the others have sold their shares to COLLINS. Before the Managers got so forward, the company (which is respectable, and many of its members from ten to eighteen years standing) *shared,* but afterwards they gave small salaries ; it is said that *Portsmouth* made their fortunes. The elegant fashionables visiting *Southampton* refused to patronise the Theatre, in consequence of its ruinous condition, and most deplorable entrance; therefore, as the lease was nearly out, on the 12th of September 1803, they commenced campaigning in another, built under the regulation of Mr. SLATER. COLLINS gave 450 guineas for St. John's Hospital, and the ground on which it stood, in *French-Street,* nearly opposite the former Theatre; the charity being discontinued, this old building furnished him with ample materials for his new one. He says this Theatre cost him 3000*l.* which, with due deference, we should suppose an error; if we give credit for 2000*l.* besides the purchase of the ground, we think it is not amiss. It has a bad Gallery; the Pit is much too low; the Stage is short; and the Boxes so near the Pit, that the lower tier resemble the Orchester Boxes of Drury Lane, the company appearing to sit below the level of the Stage. The old Theatre had this fault also; but, we acknowledge the Green Room to be good. The house holds upwards of 100*l.*; 4s. admission to the lower boxes, which have a good lobby; as have also the upper tier. Charges 23*l.* The benefit of favorite performers generally amounts to 60 or 70*l.* *Sans Souci* CHARLES was born here.

EXPLANATION OF THE PLATE.

The right hand entrance is to the Boxes, to which there are two lobbies, lighted by the only two windows in the elevation; the door on the left, is to the Pit, Gallery, and Stage ; here the old saying is verified, " spoil the ship, &c."— for the niche over each door, meant undoubtedly for Statues of Tragedy and Comedy ; and the plynth at the top for the Royal Arms, both remain blanks.

L   THEATRE,

THEATRE, PLYMOUTH.

THE Theatricals of this place claim honourable mention, at least, for their antiquity, in an age and nation where the rust of former times is held so sacred. A sort of temporary Theatre was originally constructed in *Broad Hoe-lane*, which is now the malthouse of Messrs. LANGMEADS and Co. Here, Mr. KENNEDY and his Brandy Company (most of whom died through too frequent libations of that potent liquor), exerted their professional activity. Nothing deserving of remembrance occurred till the year 1758, when ARTHUR, a Comedian of merit, at *Covent Garden*, suggested the idea of a summer venture, and procured the shells of three unfinished houses, from a Mr. KERLY, for a sharing company ; having previously obtained a promise from Messrs. JEFFERSON and DAVIES, to support his cause, until he should repay himself 480*l.* (the money to be expended in the preparations), which he accomplished in about two years. The Theatre was opened on Monday the 25th of June, with the Provoked Husband, to five and thirty pounds. To avoid losing time, they played the first three nights without a roof, being merely covered in with sail cloth. In the course of ten weeks they took 1800*l.* No half price at benefits for the first five years. In 1759, Mr. KING was engaged from *Dublin* ; and afterwards, from *Plymouth* at *Drury-Lane.* Persons conversant in the the theatrical world allow, that even in *London*, the play of The Conscious Lovers was never cast so well as in the following Bill, comprizing the united excellence of both the *London* houses.

Young Bevil......by......Mr. FLEETWOOD,
Cimberton ......by......Mr. ARTHUR,
Sir J. Bevil ......by......Mr. CLOUGH,
Tom ....by......Mr. KING,
Myrtle ....by......Mr. JEFFERSON,
Sealand ....by......Mr. DAVIES,
Humphrey ......by......Mr. COSTELLOW,
Indiana ....by......Mrs. DAVIES,
Mrs. Sealand ....by......Mrs. FERGUSON,
Lucinda ....by......Mrs. JEFFERSON,
Phillis ....by......Mrs. BRADSHAW,
Isabella..........by......Mrs. STEVENS.
And the Song by Mr. VERNON.

At

PLYMOUTH.

London, Publish'd 1 Feb.ʸ 1804 by J.Woodall, Villiers S.ᵗ Strand.

At the conclusion of the following Season, ARTHER sold the concern to Madame CAPTE DEVILLE, an eminent dancer engaged in the Company, for five hundred guineas, who appointed Mr. MATTOCKS to officiate for her. In 1761, MATTOCKS bought half of the property, which, two years afterwards, he disposed of to ANTHONY KERLY (not him before mentioned) who had purchased already the other half. The house was so crowded on SHUTER's benefit that the beam of the gallery was seen to move; two uprights were in consequence placed to support it, which remain on permanent duty at this very day. Previous to the commencement of the ensuing season, KERLY wrote to Mr. JEFFERSON, who was then performing in *Dublin*, to officiate as Manager, for which service he was to receive one third of the profits, besides his salary as a performer. He acceded, on condition that the interior should undergo alteration, which being agreed to, he sent some carpenters and painters from the Theatre, *Dublin*, before whose arrival, KERLY, the Proprietor, died. Mr. MANLEY, however, the nearest surviving relation, permitted the men to proceed. Soon afterwards Mr. JEFFERSON arrived, bringing with him the major part of the *Dublin* Company, and, to his great surprize, understood that the materials had been obtained, and the alterations conducted, entirely on the credit of his name, which was well known, and highly respected. He immediately ordered in all the bills, amounting to 261*l*. and applied for exoneration to the Heir at Law. This was refused. Mr. JEFFERSON being therefore forced to the responsibility, thought it advisable to purchase the scenery and wardrobe, which were left by will to a Mr. HUNT, and secure a lease for twenty years. He remained the sole Proprietor till 1770, when he sold one third to Mr. JOSIAH FOOTE, a butcher of *Exeter*; and another third to a Mr. WOLFE of *Pynn*, near that City. This unharmonious partnership continued till 1784, when FOOTE died, leaving half his share to JEFFERSON and his Son; and the other half, to WOLFE, in trust; which part was treated for by Mr. HUNN, a mercer of the town, who deposited 150*l*. in part of payment; but being unable to furnish the remainder, WOLFE threw him into prison; and liberated him only on condition of relinquishing his claim. In 1788, BERNARD became a part proprietor; and the firm obtained, under the new Act of Parliament, a licence. When Their Majesties went to *Weymouth* in 1789, Mrs. SUMBELL (then WELLS) made every effort to attract their attention on the Esplanade; but not succeeding, she paid ten guineas a week for the hire of a yacht, to follow them to *Plymouth*, a gun was mounted on the deck, on which she sat astride, singing " God save the King." There were at least, *four per-*

sons entertained on the evening of the 25th of June 1792, if we may believe the printed bills. In the play of Venice Preserved, their was announced

The part of Jaffier, by a Gentleman, for his Amusement.
The part of Pierre, by a Gentleman, for his Amusement.
The part of Belvidera, by a Lady, for her Amusement.
And a part of the Minuet de la Cour, by a Lady, for her Amusement.

In 1793, some dispute arising between the partners, BERNARD built a temporary wooden Theatre in *George-street*; but an accommodation taking place, the Company returned to the old Theatre, after playing a few evenings only in the new one. This season, Sir CHARLES BAMPFYLDE performed the part of Captain Brazen, in his own name publicly printed in the bills, at the head of which, appeared in conspicuous characters, these words,

"By Desire of Sir CHARLES BAMPFYLDE."

We leave our readers to determine how far the name of the character, and the nature of the action, corresponded. When JOHN KEMBLE, in performing Hamlet, repeated his entreaty to his schoolfellow to play upon the pipe, BERNARD who performed the part, replied " Well, if I must, I must;" and played the air of the Black Joke: a joke by far too black for the occasion. The Gentleman who supplied us with this article (a man of strict veracity) declared that he was present. In 1794, the song of *The Little Farthing Rushlight*, being very popular with the Gallery, INCLEDON was not suffered to proceed with his character of Lubin in the Quaker, till BERNARD had complied with the wishes of the audience, by singing it; but, what is more extraordinary, and exposes in the strongest manner, their want of musical taste, is, that in 1804, INCLEDON played at *Plymouth* for *one night only*, and was prevented from proceeding, in the very part of Lubin, on account of the clamour for that truly ridiculous and unmeaning song of " Barney leave the Girl alone." INCLEDON steped forward, and appeased the tumult, by assuring the gallery that Mr BARNEY should wait on them at the end of the first Act. In the season of 1795, BERNARD was with a Company at *Guernsey*; WOLFE was also absent; and JEFFERSON disabled by the gout, to which he has been a martyr ever since, obliged to be carried in and out. He appointed Mr. FREEMAN, a performer in the neighbourhood, to assist his son in managing the concern. Shortly afterwards WOLFE returned, and blamed JEFFERSON for the appointment; notwithstanding which, he soon assigned his share to FREEMAN, as did BERNARD, whose embarrassments made it *to him* of little value; and JEFFERSON whose infirmities rendered him incapable of looking to his interest. Finding that various

treaties

treaties were carrying on with the Manager of *Plymouth Dock*, relinquished his *third*, together with the wardrobe, scenery, &c for the sole consideration of an Annual Benefit free from all expences. Thus, Mr. FREEMAN became Proprietor of the *Plymouth* Theatre, He then renewed the lease; exchanged the name of FREEMAN for that of FOOTE; refitted the interior; and bestowed on it the epithet of *Royal*—but, on what authority is yet to be discovered: however " its a good *travelling name*, and prevents a number of troublesome enquiries." The continuation of the War proved very advantageous to him, but what encreased it was the power he possessed as a licensed Manager, over the Theatre at *Plymouth Dock* (which, BERNARD once shut up). The Proprietor of the Dock Theatre had petitioned Parliament, in January 1770, to obtain a Patent; which passed the Commons, but was rejected by the Lords: the following year it was again attempted; and again was foiled. This house is a nightly scene of riot and debauchery, notwithstanding the constant presence of the Magistrates, who use their privilege of admission not only for themselves, but for their friends, without excepting Benefits. It is an undoubted injury to the other Theatre, being no more distant than a mile and a half, which space is nearly all inhabited; and, by keeping one of the Theatres open all the year, the townsmen become indifferent to theatricals in general. FOOTE, therefore, employed his power by compelling Mr. HUGHES to yield to him the Management; and to engage his Company, &c. &c. for the Dock Season. Affairs continued in this state till July 1803, when the Bills announced that Messrs. SMITH and WINSTON had bought the property. The fact was this: Mr. FOOTE obtaining an Ensigncy in the Militia, wished to be *considered* as out of the concern; and Mr. WINSTON, to oblige him, consented to favor the report—but, some disputes arising the following year in the settling the accounts Mr. W. tired of the scheme, advertised his one third part for sale, at 600 guineas, having paid 500 for it, besides his quota of the alterations; for, previous to the opening in 1804, the whole of the interior, which was in a truly deplorable condition, was rebuilt under the immediate and sole direction of, and from a drawing made by, Mr. WINSTON. The house is now extremely light and elegant; and for its size, as perfectly complete as any out of *London*. There have been added upwards of thirty scenes, twenty of which were painted by Mr. BROMLEY. Notwithstanding the shape of the stage is such as to prevent, (generally speaking) *spectacles* from being properly represented; the Melo Drama of Valentine and Orson was got up in a style far superior to any thing that has ever been witnessed here: but even that, though highly approved of, never covered its own expences. The reason has been hinted at before. The Theatre has been

opened

opened three and four nights a week, during the Summer, and once a week, in Winter, for nearly ten years past; and the Dock Theatre, three and four nights a week, for six months, and once a week for the remainder—so that the people must be satiated. Were the lisenced Managers to exert their right, and suffer only one Theatre to be open, and that but for a moderate time, there is no doubt but that the scheme would answer. The *Plymouth* taste, like that of most other country towns is very far from a refined one; prefering buffoon- ery to the chastest acting. The audience and performers are frequently annoy- ed by the halfprice visitors, who though they dare not carry their riots to the extent practised in the neighbouring house, are still a nuisance. Mr. JEFFER- SON's benefit is always well, and fashionably attended, and we are happy to add, the last two years have been particularly lucrative. Earl MOUNT EDGE- CUMBE, whose beautiful estate here, gives the title, is always, when at his seat, the patron of the night. Mr. J. brings to the recollection of his friends, the days of GARRICK, and generally delivers such selections from one of his favourite parts, as do not require him to *stand* before them; always expe- riencing the hearty welcome that he highly merits;—he has lived here many years in a house belonging to Mr. RICHARDS, builder, next the Theatre: his bed room window is an object in the Plate. There are seven- teen years of the lease, at 43*l.* per annum, unexpired, held under General MANLEY. In March 1804, it was put up to auction, with several other build- ings, but not sold. The house holds 75*l.* at the usual prices of 3s. 2s. and 1s. The second price commences at half past eight, but does not affect the Gallery. Boxes 2s. Pit 1s and 6d. Benefit charges 21*l.* The seaon is from Easter to Michaelmas; which ought to be reversed.

DESCRIPTION OF THE PLATE.

The entrance to the Boxes is through a small room under the roof of Mr. Ri- chards' house, now included in the lease of the Theatre. The two adjoining doors under one pediment are, the furthest to the Gallery, the nearest to the Pit. The Stage entrance is by the door at the near end of the building.

THEATRE,

WINCHESTER.

London, Published 1 Feby 1808 by J. Woodfall, Villiers St Strand.

THEATRE, WINCHESTER.

THE first Company of respectability remembered in this part of the United Kingdom, was brought from London by Mr. YATES, in 1748, who occupied the Market-house. In 1760, Messrs. KEASBURY and GRIFFITHS, of the *Bath* Company, built a temporary Theatre, in consequence of a Camp consisting of eight regiments, that was formed in the neighbourhood, where they performed twelve weeks. In the play of Alexander the Great, for KEASBURY's benefit, some olive leaves that were used for decoration, twisted and interwoven with little bits of wax, caught fire from the lights. The flames continuing to blaze, occasioned an intolerable stench, and an universal cry of fire, which was succeeded by a general panic; but none received so terrible a shock as the departed Clytus, who, at that time, lay *dead* before the audience. As by Galvanic impulse, he instantly revived, and, in his haste, o'erthrew the son of the immortal Ammon, who measured his extended length on that dread spot where he had slain his General. However, as soon as the cause was ascertained, all was restored to order, and the redoubted Clytus quietly returned, and (hard and uncommon lot) for the *second* time gave up the ghost. The following season, Mr. LEE carried a Company (probably from *Portsmouth*) to *Winchester*, every Saturday for several weeks, in August or thereabout.—SHUTER, GRIMALDI, and the celebrated NANCY DAWSON were among his actors. This was continued at different succeeding periods. This Theatre was pulled down in 1763, when the Town-hall was handsomely fitted up for a Company, under the Management of Mr. SAMUEL JOHNSON, which afterwards fell into the hands of Messrs, COLLINS and DAVIS. After performing near the Cathedral over some shambles, a neat and commodious Theatre was erected by subscription, in 1785, for 1000*l.* which hold 60*l.*; 16*l.* being the expences. The subscription is now paid off, and the Theatre become the exclusive property of Mr. COLLINS.

THEATRE,

THEATRE ROYAL, NORWICH,

———

HAS the honour of being a Royal Theatre. A strolling Company occasionally performed here, from the year 1712; the particulars of which, were of too valuable a nature to be thrown away upon posterity, for which we have little doubt but that posterity has reason to be thankful. On Tuesday the 31st of January, 1759, an elegant Theatre was opened with The Way of the World, under the Management of Mr. HURST. It was built by Mr. IVORY, who has has left many proofs of his abilities in this city as an architect. Messrs GRIFFITH, BARRETT, and BRUNTON had the Theatre successively, after Mr. HURST. The *Norwich* Theatrical Fund was established the 21st of January 1791, being the only one, *Bath* excepted, out of *London :* the attempt of WILLIAMSON, at *Liverpool*, about nineteen years ago, not succeding, as recorded in our history of that Theatre. In 1799, the Management devolved on a plaisterer of the name of WILKINS. The value of this Theatre has encreased more rapidly than perhaps any of its cotemporaries; it was let to BARRETT for 180*l.* per annum; at the expiration of whose lease, BRUNTON renewed it at 300*l.*; and WILKINS agreed to take it at 750*l.* HINDES is the Manager; but is by no means equal to the task of catering for the *Norwich* apetites; the salaries are very fair, for if they have none exceeding fifty shillings, they have none (which is more essential) under five and twenty, and very few so low; this is a very profitable circuit, and deserves a freer spirited proprietor than it enjoys at present. The year is made out thus: first, *Yarmouth*, then *Ipswich*, a distance fifty-three miles; forty-three more to *Norwich* (for the Assizes); back to *Yarmouth*, twenty-two; then to *Stirbitch*, eighty-six; to *Bury*, twenty-eight; *Colchester* twenty-two; to *Ipswich* again, eighteen; to *Norwich*, forty-three; *Lynn*, forty-four; back again to *Norwich*, forty-four; and again to *Yarmouth*, twenty-two; making in the whole a very pretty twelvemonth tour.

NORWICH.

London, Publish'd 1 April 1813, by T. Woodfall, Villiers S.t Strand.